FINDING THE
RIGHT
PATH

FINDING THE
RIGHT
PATH

A GUIDE TO LEADING AND MANAGING
A TITLE INSURANCE COMPANY

ROGER LUBECK
CHRIS HANSON

FINDING THE RIGHT PATH:
A GUIDE TO LEADING AND MANAGING A TITLE INSURANCE COMPANY

Cover Design by Ted Stanaszek

Library of Congress
Cataloging-in-Publication Data Available
LCCN 2011940357

ISBN-13: 978-0983728139
ISBN-10: 0983728135
282 pages
Revised 1/15/2015

It Is What It Is Press
686 Carriage Hill Lane
Sugar Grove, Illinois, 60554
iwiipress.com

Working with
Corporate Behavior Analysts, Ltd.

"University Title Company's success today is because of practices and vision learned from working with CBA." Celia Goode-Haddock, Chairman of the Board/CEO of University Title Company, College Station, Texas.

"Engaging CBA was a turning point for Prairie Title. Roger and Chris do not come into an organization with bold promises to fix it. Instead, they teach their clients how they should think about running their businesses." Frank Pellegrini. CEO. Prairie Title, Oak Park, Illinois.

"The workshops and programs presented by CBA throughout the country have helped hundreds of independent agents meet the challenges brought about by the dynamic changes facing the title industry. Many agents consider CBA to be their 'silent partner!'" George 'Mike' Ramsey, retired in December of 2010 after 44 years in the title industry. He was a Regional Vice President and Agency Manager for Chicago and Fidelity National Title.

"With CBA's fresh set of eyes and patience we were able to develop a plan to navigate through the most difficult business climate our Industry has ever experienced. Working with them has not only been productive and enlightening, it has also been enjoyable, which helped make the entire process even more successful." Mark Myers, President, Meridian Title Company, South Bend, Indiana.

CORPORATE BEHAVIOR ANALYSTS, Ltd.

Corporate Behavior Analysts, Ltd. (CBA) is a Chicago based consulting firm providing leadership and management development. Founded in 1998 by Chris Hanson and Roger Lubeck, CBA has worked with hundreds of independent title insurance agents, the two largest title insurance underwriters, and numerous Land Title Associations. As national speakers and experts on leading title insurance companies, Roger and Chris have consulted with companies in more than thirty states.

ROGER C. LUBECK, Ph.D.

Roger Lubeck, Ph.D. is President of Corporate Behavior Analysts, Ltd, and has over 30 years of consulting experience in real estate services, healthcare, higher education, manufacturing, and mental health. Roger has a Ph.D. degree in Experimental Psychology from Utah State University and degrees in Behavioral Psychology from Western Michigan University. In his career, Roger has been a business consultant, workshop leader, retreat facilitator, public speaker, speechwriter, assistant professor, researcher, parent trainer, and dogcatcher. Roger is married to Lynette Chandler, a University Professor and author. Roger is the author of two published novels and a number of publications on customer service, leadership, management, marketing, and sales.

CHRISTOPHER R. HANSON, Ph.D.

Chris Hanson, Ph.D. is Executive Vice President of CBA. Chris holds degrees in Behavioral Systems Analysis and Clinical Psychology from West Virginia University. He has over 30 years of consulting experience in the public and private sectors. Chris has consulted with early childhood programs throughout the U.S. including establishing integrated services for HIV infected children and their families. Since 1991, Chris has advised and coached business executives and managers in the title insurance industry. He is an avid backcountry skier, loves Black & White photography, and lives in Chicago with his wife Cheriann, two daughters Lindsay and Kristan, and a black lab named Sam.

Dedication

To Lynette Chandler: Once more into the breach.
Down one more path.

To Cheriann, Lindsay, and Kristan Hanson: The home team that
keeps the light on and helps me find my way.

FINDING THE
RIGHT
PATH

A GUIDE TO LEADING AND MANAGING
A TITLE INSURANCE COMPANY

ROGER LUBECK
CHRIS HANSON

TABLE OF CONTENTS

PREFACE

FINDING OUR PATH

In writing any business / professional book, the authors have to address what the book is about, whom the book is for, and what qualifies the authors to write on the subject. This book focuses on leading and managing title insurance companies. It is a guide for owners and managers working in title insurance companies and agencies, fee attorneys, and/or escrow / settlement companies.

This book is for title insurance professionals working as managers or supervisors. We wrote it for both a new manager (first time) and for more experienced managers. It neither covers every topic found in a textbook on management nor does it present research or references on every topic. This is a book summarizing our experience and it focuses on those aspects of management that we find ourselves giving advice on repeatedly.

We have divided the book into sections on Leadership and Management. A second volume on Strategy will follow. Each chapter was written to stand on its own, but there is a logical sequence to the topics. In each chapter, we have highlighted certain guiding principles; these appear in a box in the chapter and are listed at the end of the chapter. In addition, we have included take away activities that can be completed in the office. When we conceived of the book, we thought about an owner using it with his/her managers, especially new managers. In our thinking, the management team would read one chapter and then review the chapter with his/her manager. The guiding principles are intended to stimulate a conversation among managers.

By way of background, my co-author Chris Hanson and I have worked together as full time consultants for more than nineteen years. In 1998, we started Corporate Behavior Analysts, Ltd. (CBA). At CBA, we like to say that we help clients find the right path to their business success. We use our knowledge and experience to advise and guide owners and managers in making business decisions.

In our nineteen years, we have consulted with the largest title insurance underwriters, companies with thousands of managers, and we have consulted with companies with as few as three employees. At times, we have worked together with the same client and we have each maintained our own separate set of clients. When we could, we have published articles, and presented seminars and workshops primarily on leadership, management, and sales.

In terms of background and training, we are both Ph.D. level Psychologists, meaning that we have over ten years of university training related to why people behave as they do.

Chris Hanson is a Clinical and Behavioral Systems Psychologist; he was trained to work in human service systems that provide psychological and other services to people with disabilities or people who have behavior problems related to mental illness. The systems part of Chris' training meant that he was interested in how organizations work as opposed to treating the individual. After graduating from West Virginia University, Chris directed several mental health programs, but his overriding interest was to work as a consultant in business, which he did beginning in 1991.

Roger is an Experimental Psychologist meaning he was trained to conduct research and to test theories or questions related to why people behave as they do. After completing his doctoral requirements at Utah State University, he taught Psychology at several Universities. Early in his years of university teaching, Roger began consulting with mental health agencies. In his last six years at Southern Illinois University, in addition to teaching and consulting, he managed two human service agencies whose purpose was to prevent child abuse.

In addition to the title insurance industry, we have consulted in a number of different industries and businesses, experiences that provide us with inspiration and guide our work. For example, law firms, a graphic design firm, a builder, and real estate companies. Also, we have consulted in health care: working in hospitals, physician practices, hospice facilities, and schools for chiropractic training. As a graduate student, Roger was hired as a behavior therapist at a school for the deaf. In college, Roger worked on a line at Chrysler and was a Humane Society worker (dog catcher) in Detroit. Chris sold ski equipment in New York.

In 1991, Chris joined a management-consulting firm, Corporate and Organizational Behavior Analysts (COBA). In 1992, Roger left the university world and joined Chris working for COBA. At that time,

Chicago Title Insurance Company was one of COBA's clients. In 1992, we developed and delivered a management-training program to the top tier of office managers at Chicago Title and Ticor. Following that program, we developed and delivered a similar program for a select group of top Chicago Title and Ticor agents.

In ensuing years, we have consulted with the major underwriters, we have worked with title agents in thirty states, we have conducted a seminar series for one hundred of the largest title insurance companies, and we have spoken to thousands of title insurance professionals all across America. Finally, in our day-to-day consulting, we have worked with hundreds of supervisors, managers, and owners, all in one industry, Land Title Insurance.

In summary, we have spent more than half our careers advising, working with and guiding owners and managers in title insurance companies. This book is a first pass at sharing the knowledge and experiences we have gained along the way. Along our own path to success.

Roger C. Lubeck, Ph.D.

Chris R. Hanson, Ph.D.

Acknowledgements

There are many important mentors, peers, friends, and customers who have contributed to and shaped our professional lives. For Roger, Richard W. Malott and J. Grayson Osborne were early academic mentors and continue to be friends. In terms of understanding the art of business consulting and working with the Title Insurance Industry, no persons could be more important to our development than Jon Krapfl and Jim Noah, the founders of Corporate and Organizational Behavior Analysts, Inc. COBA was our training ground and Jim and Jon were role models, mentors, and friends. We also would like to mention those industry leaders, managers, and independent title insurance agents with whom we have had the pleasure to work. Of special note are Chris Abbinante, Amy Everett, and Susan Tempest for their contributions to the book. In addition, we want to thank Alan, Allen, Betsy, Bill, Bob, Burt, Buzz, Celia, Chris, Dave, Debbie, Debi, Diane, Dick, Don, Frank, Gary, Jack, John, Ken, Larry, Linda, Louis, Margaret, Marion, Mark, Molly, Nancy, Peter, Renee, Robin, Scott, Stat, Steve, Susan, Ted, Terry, Wanda, and all the others. You know who you are and we thank you, because without your desire to develop and improve your organizations, this book would not have been possible.

LEADERSHIP

FINDING THE RIGHT PATH

This book is about leading and managing a title insurance company. In this chapter, we examine those aspects about leadership and management that are common to any business and we consider why leading and managing a title insurance company requires certain unique skills, experience, and knowledge. In Chapter 2, we provide an overview of the title insurance industry and our perspective on leading and managing a title insurance company in the future.

For the majority of the 20th century, business schools of management have argued that "management is management," meaning if you learned certain basic principles of management, including analyzing facts, making decisions, and solving problems you will be able to manage any company. In this approach, if you have a business degree, a degree in management, you should be able to manage a restaurant, a clothing store, a manufacturing company, or a title insurance company.

For years, we bought into the general manager concept, and we focused on a set of business skills that every manager needs. However, in twenty years of consulting in the title insurance industry, we have met very few managers with a degree in management and even fewer who accepted the idea of a general manager in a title insurance company. Rather, they believed managing title insurance employees: searchers, examiners, processors, and closers require specific technical knowledge and managing such technical people is different from managing employees in any non-technical business.

Today, we have come to believe that the first requirement for leading and managing is having good people skills. Effective leaders and managers are able to direct, influence, motivate and support their employees. They are skilled at the people side of the business. In addition, we have come to believe that managing a title insurance company requires specific technical knowledge, and experiences in addition to the ability to influence people and work. Finally, we recognize that creating a sound business, making a profit, and getting results the right way is an essential requirement for any leader. In a title insurance company, the most successful people we know combine all three of these dimensions. In essence, we have concluded that leading and managing a title insurance company and title employees is different from other small businesses in part because of its technical nature and in part because of having technical employees. If you are a title insurance professional, we did not have to convince you that a title insurance company is different and perhaps unique. What may be harder to get you to understand and accept is the idea there are leadership and business processes and tools you may not have but you will need in the future.

In this book, we address many of the business skills we feel title insurance company leaders and managers always need or will need in the future. Most of these processes and skills are not new. We have been talking about them for years. What is different is we are explaining them based on our experience in the title insurance industry and using examples from actual title insurance companies.

Guiding Principle

> *Leading and managing a title insurance company requires good people skills and technical knowledge and experience.*

If you are the owner of a title insurance company, we already know several things about you. First, unless you are a silent partner and only in it for the money, you have worked in the title business, you like the title insurance business, and you were successful, otherwise why select this industry as a business. If you have worked successfully in a title insurance company you either have a technical background (title or escrow) or you can sell, or both.

The next thing we might guess is you did not like working for someone else, perhaps you like to be in control. Finally, no matter how careful or conservative your nature, we know as an owner that you are willing to take on a level of risk that is greater than most people in business. So far, these guesses did not require a degree in psychology and neither does this last guess. If you have been in business for more than three years and are making money, we know you are doing something right. On the other hand, if you have been in business more than three years and are losing money, we know you are in trouble and if something does not change and improve, you will be out of business. In simple terms, if you are losing money, you are following the wrong path and you need help to find the right path to your future success.

At some point, every business owner, leader or manager needs outside advice, whether legal, financial, technological, or human resources. Smart owners seek advice before they even begin and they obtain professional advice throughout the company's lifetime. Unfortunately, many owners wait until the business is in ruins before they ask for help. Look at the cover of this book. It is a picture of a blue marble making its way through a wooden Labyrinth puzzle. If you had one of these games, you know it is easy to find yourself in a dead end and it is easy to take a wrong turn or make a wrong move and have the bottom drop right out from under you. Being the leader or manager of a title insurance company is a lot like this game. One wrong move and you are out, and even when you successfully get past one hurtle, there is always another one.

Expectations of Leaders

To be an effective leader, you have to understand the job requirements and the roles you will play. In a small business, one difficulty in understanding the job of the owner is the owner is likely to play the roles of leader, manager, and primary employee. In a small independent title insurance agency, for example, the owner is expected to be the leader and office manager. He/she also may serve as the lead salesperson, examiner, or closer. At the end of the day, the owner is probably the person who locks up at night and takes out the trash. In a small business, having to be a leader one day, and a manager the next, and co-worker throughout the week can be confusing.

Guiding Principle

> ***Acting as leader, manager, and team member is confusing.***

One way to reduce this confusion is to be clear about what is expected in each role. The job of a leader is perhaps the most difficult because we do not do it every day, but when we need to lead, acting like a manager or employee will not do. Providing leadership can mean

3

many different things because different situations require different styles and types of leadership.

Guiding Principle

> **Leaders provide direction, inspiration, and motivation.**

Every business leader has these expectations:

1. Provide direction.
2. Establish the values and vision.
3. Set goals and standards.
4. Look out for employees.
5. Inspire and motivate.
6. Solve problems.
7. Promote innovation and change.
8. Keep the company informed.
9. Promote the company with customers/community.
10. Ensure the financial stability of the company.

If you are the manager of a company owned by someone else, or you manage an office owned by a large company, you might not have a role in establishing values and vision or use your own money to keep the company going, but other than these differences, every leader is expected to demonstrate these qualities when necessary.

Leadership Style

Whenever Psychologists analyze people, they have a tendency to divide the people and behaviors into categories. For example, there are various models of leadership, which describe the style or approach taken by different leaders. For several years, we have used two different Inscape publishing tools to describe and categorize a person's basic behavioral profile (DiSC), and his/her Dimensions of Leadership Profile.

In the Dimensions of Leadership Profile, people lead by using one of four major styles: Character, Analysis, Interaction, or Accomplishment. For example, a leader who leads by Character may be respected for her integrity and enthusiasm. People respect a leader known for her Analysis because she shows good judgment and is perceptive. A leader known for Accomplishment is likely to be bold and focused on performance and results. Finally, a leader known for Interactions leads by inspiring, serving others, and collaborating.

In looking at leadership styles, there is no question a person can try to lead from various different styles. However, it also is true that most people have a preferred or natural style and in difficult situations, they are likely to fall back and rely on one style. Knowing what style (if any) you use and understanding when this style is useful and what to watch out for can be invaluable for any leader.

For example, a person who leads by Character sets a high regard for his values and will hire people with similar values. This is a person, who does what he says. He is honest and viewed as incorruptible. People who will follow this leader are likely to share his or her values. People will follow this person because they have come to trust what he says and does. They respect him. This leader fails if his followers call into question his values, integrity, or honesty. This person will fail as a leader if people learn they cannot trust what the person says or does.

Consider a different leader, one who leads by Interactions. This leader sets a high value on collaboration and teamwork. This person puts herself after others. She is a servant leader, meaning her job is to represent, to serve her employees. This leader inspires and makes others feel inspired. She asks the question, 'What can I do for you?' People follow this leader because they feel underrepresented, and this leader speaks for them. The difficulty for this leadership style is that it is easy to tell rather than listen, and easy to make decisions without input.

As Psychologists, we tend to believe leadership is situational, meaning that different situations require different styles. However, there are certain critical jobs every leader must do regardless of style. Whether you are values driven or analytic, new to leadership or have been running a business for twenty years, what is important to understand is the primary job of the leader is to create a business that is profitable, a business that is growing. Beyond profit, the job of the leader is providing direction that brings about innovation and change.

Guiding Principle

> **Leadership is about change.**

More than any other time or situation, leadership is required when something has to change. On a day-to-day basis, employees do not need or expect leadership. Rather, they need management and teamwork. People need leadership when the company is trying to change. Leadership is needed when internal problems or external factors are threatening the company. In Chapters 2-5, we consider four aspects of leadership:

Leadership Chapters
2. Understanding the title industry as a business.
3. Assessing your organization.
4. Setting direction.
5. Using measures and metrics.

We chose to focus on these dimensions because they are essentials for leading a title insurance company. In Chapters 6-13, we examine eight aspects of management:

Management Chapters
6. Developing a team.
7. Employee culture.
8. Starting to manage.
9. Influencing behavior.
10. Setting expectations.
11. Supportive coaching.
12. Managing problems.
13. Why meetings are important.

In Chapter 14, we examine how to make change practical. Deciding to change and designing change is essentially an issue of leadership, however, ultimately causing change is the task of the manager.

Management

The primary job of the manager is to create stability at work. The manager's job is to organize and manage the way work is performed. In all companies, the role of every employee is to perform the work for which he/she is paid, to meet the standards for their job, to abide by the policies of the company, and represent the values of the company at work. Finally, every employee should have a role in achieving the goals of the company.

A manager's expectations should be about the work and the employees. To that end, a manager has to ensure:

- The work is timely.
- The work is complete.
- We are productive as a team.
- We are accurate as a team.
- We meet our goals.
- Cooperation within and between units.
- We are improving.

In addition, a manager has to ensure that:

- The work is covered.
- Employees show up.
- Employees show up on time.
- Employees follow procedures.
- Employees abide by policies.
- Employees respect one another.
- Employees get along.
- We have fun.

The job of the manager is to ensure that others produce and deliver the products and services of the company. The manager has to ensure that the products and services meet industry and company standards. All of this must be done while managing expenses. In the end, the expectation of the manager is to return an adequate profit.

Guiding Principle

> ***Managers create a stable work environment.***

When needed, the manager has to take off his/her manager hat and become another team member, examining files or closing deals. At other times, the manager has to provide leadership. However, this is not an everyday job.

Finding your path

One of the great things about America is that an entrepreneur can make money in all kinds of ways. It is also one of the biggest challenges. We once heard a speaker talk about the right way to manage and the wrong way. Unfortunately, in recent years, a small number of very successful businesses brought all of the real estate related industries (including title insurance) to their knees because they were mismanaged. Managed the wrong way, the CEOs and Boards of Directors allowed money and greed to drive their business. One thing we have learned is making money is never sufficient evidence that a business is managed the right way.

Many small businesses start up and succeed almost by accident. Have you ever been in a small local restaurant where, in your opinion, the food is great, the service superior, and the sense of hospitality created by the family that owns the restaurant is welcoming and makes you want to come back? Getting it right in the restaurant business may be very different from getting it right in the title business, but when an owner gets it right in any industry, he is tempted to do one of two things, sell or expand.

Think about your favorite hole in the wall restaurant. Often times, after a period of success the owner of a successful small business will move into new space, tripling the number of tables, adding a bar, and hiring a dozen new staff. Other owners, following the success of their business, will open a second location. If you have seen this happen to your favorite restaurant, the question is what happened next. For many small businesses, expanding or adding locations means they stop doing what they do best and fail. Did this happen to your favorite restaurant? Was the new location packed at first with customers who seemingly loved the restaurant, but then because it was too crowded, the regulars dropped off, and then because revenue was down, the owner cut back on the quality of the food, and the service became indifferent? Over time, as fewer and fewer customers arrived for dinner, did the owner fire all the employees who were not relatives, until the owner went broke and closed the doors? Do you know a business with a story like this?

Today, according to Small Business Administration statistics fifty one percent of businesses make it five years, but that means forty-nine percent close their doors before five years. Why? As a business grows, the owner is faced with a series of business decisions related to location, management, products, services, customers, employees, facilities, technology, sales, etc. Just like moving through the puzzle.

As business psychologists, we could have written a general business book on leadership and management, but hundreds of such books exist and most take their ideas from books by a few leading writers, like, Peter Drucker and Jim Collins. Rather than write another general book we decided to discuss what we know best, title insurance companies. Now all that remains is to convince you that our experience and expertise, our advice will be helpful for you. Perhaps an example will help.

Several years ago, we worked in a title insurance company that was losing more than $15,000 a month due to escrow errors. Errors that were being made by employees. This was a large company and $15,000 a month was a small percentage of total revenue. When we met with the owner, he made it clear he wanted to 'stop the bleeding,' however, he was very aware of the sensitivity of the manager in question. In essence, the owner did not want to upset the manager.

When we met with the office manager, he assured us, and his boss, that his claims were declining and he had the problem well in hand. In essence, he said he did not need our help. As such, we moved on. After a year with off and on again losses, we were called in again to correct the problem that now included a $90,000.00 claim.

To start, we did something the owner and manager had not done, we examined in detail the company's claims records. We mention this because one of the things we have learned is we are often hired to do something the company could have and should have done, but did not take the time to do. In this case, we analyzed and solved the problem in a matter of days.

Based on our claims analysis, we determined that over 80% of the losses were due to the same small type of errors (less than five). We also discovered that the same three employees, mostly caused the losses. Fortunately, by the time we arrived on site, the three employees no longer worked for the company and most of the problem had corrected itself, because new employees with better training and knowledge of local practices were working in the office. Nonetheless, the mistakes made by the past employee were still costing the company money, which might have been saved had we started sooner.

In the end, we spent two afternoons working with the manager and the new employees to establish procedures to avoid the types of errors that had been so costly in the past. In essence, we established a set of rules and procedures designed to avoid the common mistakes made in that specific market.

Although we consider this case as a success, it offers an important lesson for anyone in the title insurance business. Title companies are in the business of reducing risks. When we initially proposed what we wanted to do, the owners decided to hold off and not take advantage of our assistance for two reasons. One, they thought they could correct the problem themselves, and two, they did not want to spend more money on top of what they were already losing.

On paper, their reasoning was sound, but we knew they were wrong. First, the manager of that office was a significant moneymaker and was confident he could solve problem without outside help. Second, even with its losses the office in question was one of the most profitable offices in the company, so it was argued, the losses, as a percentage of revenue, could be written off as a cost of doing business. Finally, the company had a dozen other successful managers and offices, so the owners reasoned, they had ample internal experience to draw from and could send in one of their own to solve the problem even if the manager in question failed and had to be replaced.

This example, provides an insight into this specific company that sets it apart from most other title insurance companies and from any well-managed business. The goal of every business is to make a profit. Title companies have the added responsibility to reduce risk. As such, escrow loses that are the result of controllable errors become a failure of leadership and management. From our point of view, this example is important because it illuminates a number of problems we have encountered in consulting with any business.

In this case, the owner wanted the office manager to dig his way out of a problem he had caused. To assist the manager, the owner had monthly meetings to review progress and he offered himself and other managers as go to the experts. In offering this assistance, the owner believed he was giving the manager the necessary tools to turn around the problem. The trouble was there was no analysis of the problem, there was no plan to change the problem, and there was no one responsible for or dedicated to solving the problem. A year, and some $250,000 later, we were called back in by the owner because he was still losing money and he was ready to fire the manager. In essence the owner had taken a wrong turn down a dead end and he was about to lose the blue marble.

Once we were back on site, we spent several days observing the office workflow and analyzing loss data. Using the help of the manager and several key employees, we went back through a year of claims data and categorized each claim into one of ten types. Based on this analysis, we identified the most common errors and determined that the majority of claims were caused by a small number of mistakes (i.e., The Pareto principle or 80/20 rule). Armed with this analysis, the employees and the manager designed a set of procedures to avoid these mistakes in the future. In a matter of days, we solved a problem that the manager and the company had not solved in two years. Why? Because we knew the problem was the manager, the way he had organized the work, and how he managed people and performance. Does this example prove that managing a title insurance company is unique? Not really. The manager's problems stemmed from a lack of communication, a tendency to do everything himself, everything at the last minute, and a failure to supervise and correct the work of others, all problems we have seen in other types of companies. What makes this example important is solving the problem quickly required a specialized knowledge of the industry and local practices, knowledge of claims management and analysis, and knowledge of what level of loss was acceptable or standard in the industry. The knowledge that we had as title insurance industry consultants was knowledge the manager did not possess, even with years of experience in the title business. Knowledge not taught in law school.

As a business grows there are any number of steps that can be taken on the path to success. At a certain size, every owner will need others to manage the work. At a certain size, the business needs systems rather than heroes. At a certain size, the business will have to have an infrastructure that supports the purpose of the business. At CBA, our role is to assist owners and managers in making certain key decisions throughout the lifetime of the business. As a leader and manager, your job is to find the right path to success. Our job is to help.

TAKE AWAY ACTIVITY
CHAPTER 1
FINDING THE RIGHT PATH

1. How has your organization changed in the last two years?

2. List any critical decisions you must make in the next two years.

3. Examine the list of tasks, issues, and problems and identify whether the situation call for leadership, management, or teamwork.

[L / M / T] A competitor is offering a new service.

[L / M / T] An employee is under producing.

[L / M / T] An employee is drinking at lunch.

[L / M / T] Escrow losses are up.

[L / M / T] The budget is overdue.

[L / M / T] Employee reviews are overdue.

[L / M / T] A manager is criticizing customers.

[L / M / T] An employee is having trouble at home.

[L / M / T] Calling a customer to address a complaint.

[L / M / T] A sales person is over promising to the customer.

[L / M / T] A closer is accepting gifts from a customer.

[L / M / T] The reason for a new computer system is explained

[L / M / T] Employees need to be held accountable for policies

[L / M / T] Setting a new dress code

[L / M / T] Targeting new customers

[L / M / T] New Employee Training

[L / M / T] Implementing a new computer system

GUIDING PRINCIPLES
CHAPTER 1
FINDING THE RIGHT PATH

1. Leading and managing a title insurance company requires good people skills and technical knowledge and experience.

2. Acting as leader, manager, and team member is confusing.

3. Leaders provide direction, inspiration, and motivation.

4. Leadership is about change.

5. Managers create a stable work environment.

THE BUSINESS OF TITLE INSURANCE

In this overview, we consider what sets title insurance apart from other insurance and what makes it different to manage from other types of professional businesses. Before we talk about the title insurance industry, it is important to recognize the different types of title insurance companies that exist in the United States. One distinction is between companies owned by one of the major underwriters as contrasted with independent title insurance agencies. For the most part an independent title insurance agency will be licensed or approved by one or more underwriter so they do have a connection to the larger company, but an underwriter does not own them and they usually have more than one underwriter.

Another difference is the type of company, for example. S Corporation, C-Corporation, Professional Corporation, or Professional Limited Liability Corporations. While these are tax distinctions, Law firms with a title insurance company often are PC or PLLC whereas title insurance companies without attorney owners are seldom Professional Corporations. In our experience, the difference between an attorney owned company and a corporation without attorney owners is significant in that most title insurance companies owned by attorneys are managed like law firms.

In small businesses, size is important. The definition of a small business is that it is independently owned, it is in business for profit and it is not dominate in its market or industry. Clearly, a privately owned company with five employees is a small business, but so is a company with 200 employees and revenue of ten million dollars. So, are you a small business or a really small business?

In our experience, companies with one to fifteen employees are different from companies with twenty-five to fifty employees, and companies with more than one hundred employees are different still. A related distinction is the number of offices being led and managed.

A company with fifty employees in one location is different from a company with fifty employees in seven offices.

Regardless of the company's overall size, an office with seven employees will have leadership and management issues common to any other business of the same size regardless of how big the parent company. Likewise, an office of twenty-five will have different problems from an office of five and share much in common with any title insurance company of the same size. Primarily, leading and managing are about people. The more people you have to lead and manage the more issues and problems.

Guiding Principle

Leading and managing are about people

Finally, we have to say something about family businesses. We just said that a business with five people is the same regardless of the size of the parent company. This is true provided the owners of the company are not the actual parents. Small family businesses have all the problems of any small business and on top of that, they have the problems of being a family. A small business often needs professional help and sometimes business counseling. A Family business invariably needs some level of family counseling too.

The Title Insurance Industry

In a real estate transaction, the title insurance company determines (or perhaps assures) whether a piece of real property is free of any liens or defects so that it can make a commitment to issue a policy that will insure the property being sold (transferred). The title insurance policy covers any defects in the chain of title that existed before the sale of the property, meaning problems or issues related to the property or its ownership prior to the sale. These problems could exist because they were missed in the abstracting and examination of the chain of ownership or because of errors in the records related to the property and its owners. In essence, a title insurance policy is insuring the past.

In some ways, it is similar to the warranty on a car, in that it is insuring the owner against defects that actually occurred in the manufacture of the product but are not discovered until after the sale.

This statement is so important to understanding title insurance from other insurance that perhaps we should say it again. Title insurance insures the past. All other insurance insures the future, they insure against the chance of some event in the future. Title insurance guards against errors of omission and commission made in searching and examining a property's records. Life insurance, for example, assumes a certain level of risk. Title insurance is trying to avoid, reduce, or eliminate risk.

Guiding Principle

> *Title insurance insures the past.*

In early America, the transfer or conveyance of property was performed by attorneys. In the early days in the United States, when a piece of real property was sold, the seller and the buyer were usually both represented by attorneys. If a bank loaned money for the sale, then the bank's attorney or a bank representative might be involved too. In the sale of property, the attorneys were employed to draw up the purchase agreement and to assure the property was owned by the seller and the property was free of any liens or other issues (problems or defects in title) that would prevent the sale. At this time, the attorney or a company would abstract the property records, examine the records, and then offer an opinion regarding the salability of the property.

In the late 1800's, companies like Chicago Title came into existence. Initially, these companies were successful because of the quality of their independent land records. After the Great Chicago Fire of 1871, it was the independent land records of three companies that became the basis for Cook County's land records.

At first, these businesses sold title evidence to other attorneys who then examined the abstracted evidence of ownership, offered a legal opinion and performed the settlement. By 1888, title insurance companies were issuing a title insurance policy, meaning that the company would stand behind the accuracy of its title work if there were a claim regarding ownership. The policy would protect the buyer against the claim. Over time, the most successful of these companies became today's major insurance underwriters and title agents.

Different Insurance

When a person takes out a term life insurance policy, he/she is buying a policy that assures money will be paid if the insured dies during the term of the policy. An insurance premium is paid on some regular basis, monthly, annually, but at the end of the term, the policy has no cash value. This type of policy protects against an unexpected event. In this instance, the company issuing the insurance policy is assuming a certain level of risk.

Likewise, homeowners insurance protects against damage or loss of a house and its holdings against an unexpected event. Auto insurance protects the driver and the vehicle against an unexpected event during the term of the policy. In some sense, all of these other insurance policies are a wager, a bet between the insurance company and the policyholder. The price of the policy is based on an actuarial model or a statistical database that describes the incident of the insured event (accident) or claims over time. Based on these actuarial statistics, the insurance company calculates a price for a policy with the intent to fund all claims, cover business costs, and to make a profit. The purpose of an insurance company is to assume the risk on the part of the customers it insures, and make a profit doing so.

The cost of insurance is determined using statistics to determine risk and taking into account the cost of doing business. In some states the price is set by the state, and in other states, the insurance company can set the fee. In either case, the fee is highly competitive because the science behind pricing the risk is well established and standardized. For example, today most homeowners insure their home and automobiles and other valuables through a single insurance agent like Famers, or State Farm, or that company with the Gecko, Geico. They also may have life insurance policies with one of these companies. What they do not have with any of these national carriers is title insurance. Life, Property, and Casualty (P & C) Insurance are regulated by each state and sold by local agents, but these agents have not, and in some states cannot sell title insurance because title insurance is fundamentally different from P & C Insurance.

As we stated earlier, title insurance protects the owner of the property against problems or defects in title. The fee for the policy is paid once at closing and it protects the buyer against problems in the land records that were not discovered at the time of the transference of property. The title policy assures protection and the title insurance company is assuring that they will defend the owner and cover any legal costs if there is a claim. In actuarial terms, the price for a policy is based on the company's claims history, which is a reflection of the quality of the records, abstracting, examination, and underwriters, meaning the company' accuracy in discovering problems in the title. In essence, the title insurance company is betting that the records they are using are correct and that they did not make a mistake in checking the records.

When we compare title insurance to other insurance, the purpose of title insurance is to reduce or eliminate the risk in buying real property. In terms of managing a business, the quality of work performed by the title examiner and the settlement staff has everything to do with the level of claims. In a P & C company, the risk being insured is based on the policyholder and has almost nothing to do with the quality of the work being performed by the people working in the insurance office.

Historically, the P & C office is a sale site with no on-site (local) underwriting. In contrast, the title office is both a sales office and an underwriter; the risk is determined by work performed in the local office. This difference is one of the reasons why leading and managing a title insurance company has been different from other insurance business. Life, property, and casualty insurance protect against some future event, an event that will happen with some probability. In managing a life insurance office, the accuracy with which an employee enrolls a policyholder is important, but more important is being friendly, helpful, and customer oriented. In a life insurance office, when a claim occurs, no one is at fault. The life insurance company has assumed some level of risk and now it has to pay out. In a title insurance company, major mistakes, if made by the local company (employees) can close the business.

In the past decade, the major underwriters have taken steps to consolidate the process of searching, examining, and underwriting. Now, instead of every office performing the title production process, there are regional centers where the work is centralized. In addition, a small percentage of residential searching and examination has been automated, meaning that the issuance of the commitment to write a policy is performed largely by artificial intelligence. These changes will dramatically affect leading and managing a title insurance company in the future.

Consumer Disconnect

If you have ever sold or purchased a new home or a condominium, you know the process of transferring ownership can be quick and simple and it can be very difficult and time consuming. The reasons why a closing is easy or difficult can be complicated. For example, the property might be difficult to search and abstract. There might be problems discovered at the last minute, the lender documents or instructions might be late, or the parties show up late. All kinds of things outside of the control of the title insurance company can make for a difficult closing, and yet, when the escrow office or title manager says they are ready to close, when they accept a closing and schedule it, any problems that occur before, during or after the closing are completely the responsibility of the title insurance company and any credit or blame will fall directly on the person managing that office.

One of the reasons why the sole responsibility will fall to the title insurance company is the fact that consumers do not understand the product and the title insurance industry. Today, most residential closings probably occur in a title insurance office. Typically, the buyer will bring a very large check made out to the company conducting the settlement, in this case a title insurance company. Since the check is made out to the title insurance company, it is natural for the consumer to think the title insurance company is charging this very large fee, but in fact, there are at least four major costs associated with closing the sale of the home: there are Realtor fees, lender fees, title insurance company fees, and attorney fees (if one is used). For the first three, if not all four, the fee for service is variable and is based on the cost of the home. For example, listed below are some of the fees paid at the closing on a $200,000.00 home in Illinois in 2010.

Sale Price	200,000
Realtor Fee	12,000
Loan origination	1,653
Closing fee	376
Title insurance	600

At the time of the closing, the homeowner might write a check to a title insurance company for $15,000.00 or more in order to purchase a home, yet only $600.00 in fees are going to the title insurance policy. Compared to the Realtor and lender fees, the title fee is relatively inexpensive, typically about .5% of the value of the property.

Legislation like the Truth in Lending Act (1968) and the Real Estate Settlement Procedures Act (1974) attempted to make the fees in a settlement fair and the source of those fees understood, but for the average consumer the fees paid at the time of the closing remain a mystery.

In part, the confusion begins with who orders the title work and who pays for the title work. In most states, the buyer pays for a portion of the title fees and yet the seller usually (by custom) chooses the title insurance company. In many cases, the Realtor, lender, or attorney will guide in the selection of the title insurance company, but this custom creates a disconnect between the buyer and the title insurance company.

From the title insurance company's perspective, the buyer and seller are one-time customers and the real customer (the repeat business) is the Realtor, loan originator, or real estate attorney. In attorney based title insurance companies, the attorney may represent the buyer or seller in other legal matters, but for the traditional corporate title insurance company, the buyer and seller are an afterthought. This problem can be compounded by the fact that the homeowner seldom sees what the title fee has purchased other than the hour he/she spends in the title office signing papers. Recent changes in the law have been attempts to make the fees more understandable to the consumer. Nonetheless, the public does not understand title insurance. In the future, if a title insurance company is to survive, if the industry is to survive, it will have to close the gap between what a consumer understands and what the agent and industry provides.

Guiding Principle

> ***Consumers do not understand the products and services provided by the title insurance industry.***

An Industry in need of Professional Standards

The title insurance is a mature industry, meaning it has been in business over 100 years and it is regulated, both at the federal level and at the state level. Key among the regulations at the federal level was the Real Estate Settlement Procedures Act (RESPA). For example, RESPA made it illegal for a title insurance company to pay a "finder's fee" to a realtor for a title order and then include the cost of that "marketing" in the price of a title policy. For the past two decades, the Department of Housing and Urban Development (HUD), Fanny Mae, Freddie MAC, and the major lenders have influenced and controlled the work of a title insurance company. For example, in 2010, HUD changed the settlement form for residential transactions and every title insurance company had to change not only their forms but also the way they processed the HUD form.

In 2010, the Dodd-Frank Wall Street Reform and Consumer Protection Act (Dodd-Frank Act) established the Consumer Financial Protection Bureau (CFPB). The mission of the Consumer Financial Protection Bureau is to "make markets for consumer financial products and services work for Americans—whether they are applying for a mortgage, choosing among credit cards, or using any number of other consumer financial products." At this point, it is unclear how this new federal entity will affect title insurance companies, however, it is certain to cause change.

To complicate the picture, at the state level, each department of insurance has specific laws restricting the way title work is performed and what can be charged for title insurance. These laws do not supersede Federal law, rather they add additional restrictions and conditions on the way the title business can be conducted in a state. For example, in some states the fees for a settlement, the owner's policy, and lender policy are regulated and have to be posted. In some states, these fees are fixed, in others a company can change its fees with written notice.

As powerful as these state and federal laws and guidelines are, at one level they have done little to shape the way the actual work of a title insurance company is performed. For example, when the new HUD forms and requirements were introduced, there was no industry standard or industry process for addressing the changes. Each underwriter and each agent had to figure out how they would change. Therefore, instead of one response or five, there were thousands. For a mature profession, it is surprising there is so little standardization. Perhaps part of the problem is historic. At one time the work performed by a title insurance company was the work of a lawyer, thus, the professional standards were those associated with being an attorney. When corporate title insurance companies emerged in the 1960s and the work was no longer restricted to attorneys, there was no profession or professional group to step in and impose standards on the new title insurance companies. There standards and values were derived from each owner.

When we started consulting in 1991, each state and region had its own regulations, customs, and practices and the only guidelines being discussed were around different interpretations of RESPA. What was most surprising to us was the fact that three companies could be doing business in the same town and yet their work processes, forms, technology, and procedures all could be different, even though the policy they issued looked the same and offered the same assurance. Even within a company, we found the procedures used by different closers were different as were the work processes from one office to the next. Only recently have there been attempts, by the major underwriters, to standardize workflow and technology within their own companies. Unfortunately, efforts to standardize across the major underwriters run the risk of violating anti-trust law or employment law, so little industry standardization exists unless developed and recommended by the American Land Title Association.

Twenty years ago when we started consulting, the title insurance industry appeared to be a local business that was on the brink of undergoing a major upheaval. When we started, there was an open war in real estate to control the customer to get to the front of the real estate transaction channel, meaning to control the placement of the order. The competitors in this war were attorneys, Realtors, lenders, and title insurance companies. Positioned at the end of the channel, the title insurance industry is still being dictated to by all who come before.

When we started consulting, it was thought that the local nature of the business was changing and the title order would eventually be controlled by a small number of regional and national players. At that time fewer and fewer title agents had exclusive underwriting contracts and the big agents were writing policies on more than a dozen national and regional underwriters. This was a boom period when refinance and relaxed lending requirements drove real estate and title insurance companies followed along.

Even during the best years, there were those who argued the bubble would burst, the underwriters would be forced to consolidate and more than half the real estate and title agents would go out of business. To some extent, after 2007, this prediction has come true. Today, over 60 percent of loans are controlled by five banks. Likewise, Fidelity National Financial and First American have acquired many of the smaller underwriters, and fewer title agents and Realtors are in business today. Yet, nearly half of the title business remains for the moment local. The question is what happens when the other shoe drops.

Twenty years ago, it was believed that in the future, each of the major banks would own one of the major title underwriters and all of the background work for commercial and residential transactions would come to be performed overseas and the closing would happen in some electronic or virtual way. Remember all of this speculation was before the internet, email, Google, and Facebook. Today, consolidation is occurring at every level. Some title work is being performed overseas, and some is being performed by artificial intelligence. Today, there are companies who own every aspect of real estate including building, real estate sales, lending, and title insurance. For example, the Title Resource Group (TRG) operates over 70 distinct brand names throughout the United States.

The fact that many title insurance agencies are locally owned has been one of the barriers to changing and standardizing the industry. It also is another reason why we believe leading and managing a title insurance company is still unique. It is unique because it is a business with specialized jobs that are not standardized; jobs that take a long time to learn; jobs that are not taught in high schools or universities; jobs where mistakes that can destroy a company. Increasingly in the United States, there are employment sectors with skilled jobs where the skills are specialized and employees with those skills are hard to find and even harder to let go. The title insurance industry may be one of those sectors.

Employee Training

If you wanted to start a small fine dining restaurant, you could run an advertisement in a local paper and easily find an experienced executive chef (leader/manager) who had been trained on the job in one or more restaurants. You also could find candidates who might have worked in fewer restaurants, but who had graduated from a culinary institute or recognized food program. In either case, the candidates, the people you select to interview will have the same basic food / cooking skills and they will have an understanding of managing the business.

Today there are no colleges or professional programs training people to work in the title insurance industry. Even the major underwriters no longer have training departments. Most of the training a title employee receives is on the job and catch as catch can. Unlike becoming a computer programmer there is no standard curriculum, no accredited courses or licenses. To complicate this problem, the major underwriters and large agents are trying to standardize work within their company through technology, but there is no standard for the industry, no common technology.

There are core jobs in the industry, jobs like Title Officer or Escrow Officer, but the experience and the time it takes to learn any of the core jobs is debatable. If you ask a title department manager, she might say it takes one to three years to be a searcher and examiner. Learning to be a competent Escrow officer certainly takes several years, and even with years of experience, a searcher or a settlement officer might not be able to work on a commercial file or work at another company.

If you are a cook, the proof is in your work, the quality of your work is immediate, observable, and measurable. If you have ever watched any of the new reality cooking shows on television, you know how easy it is to sort out a good young chief. Give him or her, a knife, and ask him/her to dice one hundred onions or prepare a Mirepoix in five minutes. These are basic skills, skills that you can test. No such basics skills tests exist in the title insurance industry because the records, the title plants, the operating systems, the requirements to close a transaction are all different. Even an experienced professional might take several weeks to learn a new system.

Guiding Principle

> **Title companies have specialized non-standardized jobs.**

When you compare being a title professional to being a lawyer or physician, each profession takes years of formal training and requires on the job experience. In each case, the practitioner is a specialist, with a unique set of skills, but the skills acquired by a lawyer or doctor can be applied anywhere in the United States, provided the practitioner becomes licensed. A licensed title examiner might be employable in other states and a licensed Escrow Officer in Texas might work as a closer in Florida or California, but they will have to learn an entire set of new (different) procedures and computer system. In the title business, there is at least one constant, the phrase, "we do not do it that way here."

Management Training

Owners and managers in independent title insurance agencies, especially in non-corporate based agencies, often have technical backgrounds or sales experience with little if any leadership or management training. People who start their company probably worked in another company, so they may have had a manager who serves as a model for their own leadership and management. In some cases, where the company is family owned, a manager may have a father or a mother who serves as a role model for leadership and management, and parent.

At least for the manager coming up in a corporate system, there are likely to be a few good role models; men and women who understood the work, who were good at managing people, and a few who understood how to run a modern business. In our experience, the owner of an independent title insurance agency probably worked in another title insurance company before starting his/her own, so they too may have had a good role model, but just as likely, they started their own company because they hated being a lawyer, examiner, or closer for someone else. Often, we meet owners/leaders who know what not to do, but they are very uncertain what to do because they have never really been a true leader or manager and they lack an adequate model.

Guiding Principle

Owners have little leadership and management training.

We have been in companies with five employees, a president and Chief Executive Officer, a Vice President and Manager of the title department, a Vice President and Manager of the closing department, a Vice President and Manager of the accounting department, and a receptionist. In other words, the company had one employee and four people called executives, three managers without any experience or people to manage. This somewhat comical situation exists in all types of small businesses, but what happens as the business grows?

In our experience, most of the employees hired in a title insurance company are trained to do a specific core function, but they have no training in managing people or performance. Successful leadership and management in a title insurance company depends upon a number of variables, including the size of operation, location and market, the use of technology, and the abilities and skills of the employees. We believe that learning to effectively lead and manage a title insurance company requires a combination of very specific technical knowledge and sound operational and business experience. Given what is at risk in a title insurance company, not every type of employee will be right and not every style of leadership or management will be right. We believe finding the right path to success in a title insurance company can be guided by adopting a set of leadership and management practices that have been developed and proven within the industry.

TAKE AWAY ACTIVITY
CHAPTER 2
THE BUSINESS OF TITLE INSURANCE

1. What makes your company unique? List those aspects that make your company different from other small businesses.

2. List those properties or features that make your company different from other title insurance companies.

3. Make a list of those instances where you have to lead and those instances where you have to manage.

GUIDING PRINCIPLES
CHAPTER 2
THE BUSINESS OF TITLE INSURANCE

1. Title insurance is different from other insurance.

2. The title insurance industry suffers from a disconnect between the product it sells and what the consumer understands about the product and the industry.

3. Title companies are a business with specialized jobs that are not standardized; jobs that take a long time to learn; jobs that are not taught in high schools or universities; they include jobs where mistakes can destroy a company.

4. Managing and leading a title insurance company is different from many other small businesses.

5. The major underwriters and title agents are trying to standardize work through technology without developing a common standard for the industry, a common technology, or common training practices.

6. Owners and managers in title insurance agencies, especially in non-corporate based agencies, typically have technical backgrounds or sales experience and have little if any leadership and management training.

CHAPTER 3

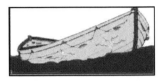

ASSESSING YOUR ORGANIZATION

In this chapter, we explore a process for assessing the strengths and weaknesses of your business and comparing your company to the threats and opportunities that exist in your market. Assessing your organization is a critical first step in determining the right path to your company's success.

Early in our careers as leadership consultants and workshop leaders, we developed a number of leadership and teamwork exercises, one of which we called the lifeboat. In part, the idea for the exercise came from movies like Alfred Hitchcock's "Lifeboat" and "Abandon Ship." Here is the synopsis of "Abandon ship."

> "After their luxury liner is sunk, a group of over twenty survivors take refuge in a life boat made for only nine. Included in the group are an old opera singer, a nuclear physicist, his wife and child, a General, a play-write and his dog, a college professor, a gambler and his mistress, the ship's nurse, and several members of the crew, including the Captain and executive officer. Soon, the captain dies from his injuries. The executive officer must take charge, and as a hurricane approaches, and their food and water run out, he must decide who to put over the side, and who stays and gets a chance at survival."

In our exercise, we select a group of employees who will go in the lifeboat and a group who will observe. The people going into the lifeboat were blindfolded and the guides were given a slip of paper with information to be given to the person in the boat once the exercise began. To create the boat, we lined up a dozen chairs in the shape of a boat, one in the stern with a rudder, then two, a row of three, and then two, and finally one in the bow. Around these chairs, we would scatter all kinds of props found on a real boat; life vests, oars, water, food, rope, compass, and some items found in a survival kit. Some of the items were in plain sight and some were hidden. Outside of the "boat", we had several spots meant to represent people in the water.

Before beginning the exercise the observers would lead a team member into a designated place in the boat or water and hand the person his/her instructions. Once everyone was in place, the exercise would begin. As facilitators, we explained the activity was designed to test the groups' leadership and teamwork. The group was told they had been on an ocean cruise liner that had exploded and sank. Each person had been thrown in the water and some had made it to the lifeboat. Their challenge was to survive. Fortunately, this was years before the TV programs like Survivor and Lost, so few of our participants had any experience with what to do in the first hour of a disaster.

In their written instructions, the people in the boat and in the water were given specific behaviors and roles to play. For example, one person was injured buy could not talk but could write. One person in the water could not swim, and did not speak English. One person in the boat had been a sailor, another was the radio operator who had sent out a distress signal, and another person had first aid training. In our instructions, some people were told they could reveal their hidden skills and others were told they had to wait until someone specifically asked about the skill.

As you might guess, once the exercise began, we added complexity to the situation by having the boat take on water or having an injured person start screaming. Invariably, the group would organize around getting people out of the water and rowing the boat. What was common to most groups we conducted was one person would stand up and take charge, assigning people to row and steer with very little assessment of the boat, its provisions or the talent and skills of the people in the boat. After a few minutes of this, we would introduce some additional significant problem, like sharks in the water, and ultimately entertaining chaos would follow.

The purpose of the lifeboat was to demonstrate that before a leader establishes goals or sets direction, he/she must assess the health of the business and the talent and skills of its employees. In the lifeboat, the team had everything it needed to survive, but most groups are unsuccessful because the person who stood up and took charge failed to assess the situation. For example, when the exercise begins, the lifeboat is taking on water. In addition, the lifeboat has large cracks on the outside of the hull that if patched immediately will not open and take on more water. In the exercise, we allowed five minutes for the team to organize and repair the boat. If they do not bail water or patch the cracks in that time, we would open the cracks and the lifeboat would sink before they could row to safety. Using our business metaphor, the message was before you try to head off in new directions, make sure the business is sound and you have an accurate assessment of your resources. Make sure you repair any weaknesses that might cause you to sink. For example, before you open a new office with an untried manager and new staff, have the new manager and staff work together in your current office.

Guiding Principle

Improve what you have first before heading in a new direction.

In some lifeboat exercises, the survivors would organize into teams: people bailing, caring for the injured, patching the boat, and rowing. For some reason, the survivors wanted to start rowing before they had any idea where they were or where they were going. It was as if any movement was good. This is a common mistake in business. For example, we have worked in companies where their prime source of revenue went away, so the company started to take on any work it could and any clients it could. In Good to Great, Jim Collin's argues that it is important for a company to stick to what it does best. He calls this the hedgehog. In title insurance companies, when refinances were up, companies went after lender clients to the point that 70% or more of their revenue came from refinances. Likewise, when the traditional real estate market disappeared, some title insurance companies went after the foreclosure market.

In each case, there is nothing wrong with going after new business, provided you have the expertise and the existing staff to conduct the business. Unfortunately, some companies were neither staffed correctly nor experienced with these different segments of business, and were put in jeopardy.

We observed this same problem with a company we work with that specialized in customizing high performance General Motors vehicles after market. When their business was down, they started accepting any vehicle, including Fords and Chryslers. Unfortunately, not all cars are engineered the same, and working on new, unfamiliar vehicles resulted in projects where the company spent more to modify the car than the customer paid for the work.

Coming back to the lifeboat, the idea is to stay where you are and improve what you have first before heading off in new directions. This is not to say that a company should not change or should not redefine its self, all we are arguing is make sure you know where you are heading and why before you start.

For example, inside a sealed envelope in a box in the lifeboat, we provided the survivors with a map and a compass. In addition, one of the survivors was secretly told he was the radio operator of the cruise liner and he knows where the ship was when it sank and he knows that a distress call went out before the ship went down. In his instructions, he was told he suffered a head injury and this information cannot be remembered unless he is asked what his job was on the boat. Using this knowledge and the tools in the boat the survivors should try to stay where they are or they could try to row or sail the lifeboat east to a larger group of islands 10 miles away. Any other action would be a waste of resources.

Organizational Review

In our practice, when we start with a company we perform an organizational review. The purpose of the organizational review is to assess the health of the company and the skills and talents of its employees. In many ways, an organization is like a living person. It goes through stages, starting out it is unsure, then with success, it begins to develop, it goes through spurts of growth, it socializes, it matures, perhaps it acquires a partner, and at some point it transforms itself or dies. Like a living person, the health of an organization can be assessed and where it is in its growth cycle can be determined.

When we review a company, we like to review everything. We look at the company's financials, we evaluate management, we assess its systems and infrastructure, we interview employees, we observe workflow, we talk to customers, and we sit in on company meetings. When we are finished, we give the owner a written report with observations, findings, and recommendations. In essence, we give the company a physical and we provide the company with a scorecard that can be compared to other title insurance companies. In many cases, our report focuses on what is missing given the company's number of employees or revenue.

For example, if you are a title insurance company with three employees it is not surprising the number of things you do not do when compared to a company of five thousand. However, if you are a company of three employees that makes five million dollars in revenue, there are certain business and accounting practices that will be essential even though you are small.

Typically in corporate title insurance companies, as opposed to law firms with a title insurance agency, there is a relationship between the number of employees and revenue. In our experience, a title insurance company will spend between 40 percent and 60 percent of its gross revenue on labor. Therefore, if a company has 10 employees and they earn an average of $40,000 a year, we can estimate that the company will have an annual revenue right around $1,000,000. With revenue of a million dollars and ten employees, there are certain business and corporate practices we expect to see, and others that while desirable would be unusual.

Now suppose we look at a ten-year-old title insurance company with 30 employees and three million dollars of revenue. Given the size of the work force and revenue, we expect this size company to have a clear organizational structure with managers and people performing accounting, human resources, and information technology. At this size, we expect some planning, an annual budget and annual goals, but we do not expect formal sales or marketing plans. There should be established procedures, work processes, and standards in place.

For example, a small company might not have a statement of vision or mission, but it should have a clear idea (written) of what business it is in, why it is in business, and what are its drivers. However, every company, regardless of size, should have an employee review process.

In our experience, predicting what business practices a company will have is a fool's errand. Unfortunately, many established and large title insurance companies have almost none of the features of a modern corporation; no meetings, no manuals, no marketing, no mission, no plans, no budget, no employee reviews, no structure, and no communication.

Guiding Principle

When you assess a company, review everything.

On the bright side, every once in a while we encounter a business with an owner who wanted to start out right and incorporate many of the good ideas a big company uses. Recently we talked with a young owner of a title insurance company with a small workforce and yet a very big revenue. This company was structured, it had all of the pieces and it was highly automated. By using technology, the company could have high volume and revenue with a very small permanent workforce. The point of these examples is rather than assume how good a company is based only on its lobby or balance sheet; we ask a series of critical questions to assess the state of the company.

In our review, we consider ten dimensions:

1. Leadership and direction.
2. Management ability and practices.
3. Financial performance / health.
4. Operational performance / health.
5. Staffing and employee culture / morale.
6. Customer service and customer satisfaction.
7. Sales and marketing.
8. Infrastructure.
9. Technology.
10. Planning and path.

Assessing Leadership and Direction

If the owner of a company works in the company then she/he will naturally be expected to be the leader, even if there are others who are appointed or hired to lead the company.

In title insurance companies, because of the technical aspects of the business, leaders are typically expected to be the most knowledgeable and certainly have the final say in any business decision. Generally, because of the behavioral characteristics of the typical title or escrow person, the employees want structure and procedures and often expect to be told what to do.

Although there are various styles of leadership, in title insurance companies we often encounter owners / leaders who appear to be very egocentric. For example, the company revolves around the owner and he/she has to be in control. Such leaders are often heroes to their customers, but may not be heroes to their employees.

Jim Collins in his groundbreaking book Good-to-Great[1] argues that the leadership quality he found most often in great companies was the steady, humble, servant leader. This is a leader who asks, "What can I do to make you (the employee) successful?" He or she is inspiring, not because of oratory, but often because his/her personal story and accomplishments leave others speechless. Unfortunately, in the hundreds of managers and leaders we have met, only a very few exhibit this style of management.

In our company, we often use the DiSC® (Inscape) to describe basic behavioral styles, as well as management and leadership styles. In title insurance agencies, the majority of employees we have encountered have steady or conscientious styles, meaning they are careful people who want structure and procedures at work. When these employees advance to management positions they continue to manage from this low key, do everything yourself style. In contrast, in corporate title insurance companies, managers who advance are usually selected because they have direct styles and get results. This more aggressive self-centered style is perfect for moving up the ladder, but as Collin's points out, such egocentric leaders seldom build companies to last.

In the DiSC system, there are eight approaches to leadership. They are Affirming, Commanding, Deliberate, Energizing, Humble, Inclusive, Pioneering, and Resolute. In these terms, the majority of corporate vice presidents we have encountered would be a mix of commanding, resolute, and deliberate. Among the homegrown managers, we have met in title insurance agencies, being deliberate, resolute, and humble may be more common. What we seldom see are managers who are Pioneering and Energizing.

In Chapter 1, we said leadership is about creating change and management is about establishing stability. For the manager of a title department or the manager of an escrow team, the nature of the work, the composition of the team, and the demands of customers are more than enough to worry about, but as leaders, these managers must be

---

[1] Jim Collins. *Good to Great. New York, HarperCollins, 2001. pp. 12-13.*

able to realize the owner's goals, both short and long term. In the ideal world, the owner's goals would determine the people who are selected to lead and manage, but in the title insurance industry, it is often the opposite. The owner has goals that the leadership and management are incapable of enacting.

In our assessment of companies, we start by determining the basic behavioral styles of owners and managers, then we examine the company's short and long-term goals and only then do we assess the workforce and its leadership and management. At this stage, we want to answer the following questions:

1. What are the owner's overall goals?
2. What are the long-term (three to five years) goals for the company?
3. What are the current (annual) goals for the company?
4. For this year, what are the company's financial goals with respect to:
    - Gross income
    - Expenses
    - Pre-tax Profit
    - Profit margin
5. For this year, what are the company's operational goals with respect to:
    - Orders per month
    - Closings per month
    - FTEs
    - Order per FTE
    - Closings per FTE

In talking with owners, we want to determine any plans to retire and what will happen to the company if the owners retire or die. Often times in small businesses, most of these questions are unanswered. For example, we like to determine, what the company will look like in three or five years for the owner(s). We ask if the owner has a vision for the future. In addition, we explore what values are important to the owner and what values are emphasized in the company. Finally, we ask the owners to identify all of the company's strengths and assets along with its deficits and weaknesses. Included in this discussion are any problems, unresolved issues, or needs. Listed below are the types of questions we would ask the owner(s).

Leadership / Owner Questions

1. What is the status of your long-term goals, are they being met?
2. What is the status of your short term/ annual goals, are they being met?
3. When do you plan to retire and what will you want to do with the company?
4. What are current levels of performance for each financial and operational goal (measure)?
5. What is your vision for the future? What vision do you have for the company?
6. What will the company look like in three years from now? Five years?
7. How would you define the company being successful?
8. What are your issues? Are they being solved?
9. What are your needs?
10. How is the company described on the street, its reputation?
11. How would you describe the company's values?
12. What are the company's strengths?
13. What are the company's weaknesses?
14. How are the company's expectations communicated to management and to staff?
15. What are the expectations of the executives in the company?
16. How have expectations been communicated?
17. How do you evaluate management performance? What criteria do you use?
18. How do you evaluate the overall performance of the title operations?
19. How do you evaluate the overall performance of the Escrow operations?
20. List each manager strength's and needs
21. How do you manage your executives?
22. How do you manage your managers?
23. How do you manage the title operations?
24. How do you manage the escrow operations?
25. How do you manage the administrative functions?
26. What information is regularly reported to the owners, executives, managers, and employees?
27. How are employees and managers compensated?
28. What operational issues do you feel exist?

In identifying vision and values, strengths and weaknesses, it is important to determine what executives and managers believe and then contrast that with what we find. Oftentimes, an owner will say that he values quality and doing it right, and then we learn that getting a commitment out, even an incorrect one is more important than doing it right the first time. Likewise, an owner may say he has the fastest turn time or the best service only to learn the company is solidly in the middle of the pack.

When we get to the operational level of a company, we like to observe the work and talk to managers and the employees they supervise. In observing work, we want to understand how an order moves through the company. If there are different offices, we focus on what procedures are the same and which are different and why. When we talk with employees, these discussions are confidential and best done one on one. Conversations with employees focus on work culture, meaning "the way we do things around here." If a company is so large that it is impractical to talk with all the employees, we will conduct a survey designed to give us a picture of Employee Culture.

Often times the patterns of behavior among employees that have evolved over time will be different from the values expressed by the owners. For example, the owner emphasizes fast service and the title department emphasizes accuracy over speed. When such differences exist, we say that a company is out of alignment. Often in developing a path for a company to follow, we are trying to align the operation with the vision of the company. Alignment occurs when the actions of the managers and the behavior of employees produces results consistent with the values and vision of the leadership.

Guiding Principle

> **Alignment occurs when managers and employees produce results consistent with the values and vision of the company.**

In title insurance companies, there are at least three distinct groups, title employees, escrow employees, and sales. In smaller companies, the owners do most or all of the sales. As companies increase in size, they will take on a permanent sales staff. In the title business, there is real confusion (lack of separation) between marketing and sales. In part, the problem is the price for a policy cannot be negotiated in most states. Setting and discounting price is one of the critical tools in sales. Without the ability to negotiate price and to sign sales agreements, the average sales person is left with sales strategies like coverage (asking) and building relationship and marketing strategies that promote the company, product quality, and service. Listed below are questions we ask about marketing and sales.

Marketing and Sales Questions

1. How would you like to see the company marketed?
2. What growth do you anticipate in the future?
3. Who are your current customers?
4. Who is your competition?
5. What are your competitors' strengths\weaknesses?
6. What gives you a competitive advantage?
7. How you would rate your operations on service?
8. What are your strategies for the future?
9. What are your issues concerning marketing and business development?
10. What is the marketing and sales approach?
11. Do you have a formal marketing plan or sales plan?
12. Do you divide your customers and potential customers into groups or segments?
13. What customer groups do you target?
14. For each customer segment do you track\monitor your sales?
15. Do you know who gives you 80% of your business in each customer group?
16. What do you feel makes this company competitive? What competitive advantage do you have?
17. What are your marketing strategies\tactics\sales tactics?
18. How do you evaluate marketing\sales tactics?
19. How much time per week do you spend on marketing\sales?
20. Who else engages in marketing\sales tactics? What do they do? How much time do they spend?
21. What are your biggest challenges regarding sales?
22. What issues do you have with operations that affect sales?

In this chapter, we described the lifeboat exercise. In the lifeboat, employees and managers are cast adrift in a sinking lifeboat. In the boat they have everything they need to survive and they have all the tools necessary for setting direction, yet, in most groups they fail to use those tools and they set off rowing even before they have a clue where they are going. Often, the reason the team is rowing is because whoever "takes charge" is the type of person who believes it is always better to be moving than to stay where you are. However, in an actual lifeboat, like life, sometimes it is smarter to sit and gather your resources and wait for help.

The point of the lifeboat exercise is before you start rowing, the leader of a ship needs to assess his/her situation. What do we know? Where am I? What are our physical assets? What are the strengths and weaknesses of our team? What are potential threats? We called this assessment an organizational review. Conceptually, this analysis could be organized into a SWOT analysis as first described by Albert S. Humphrey.

Whatever we call it, most small business, most title insurance companies need to assess their strengths and weaknesses honestly before adopting a new computer system or opening a new office. In our experience, many title insurance companies do not know where they are headed, and even when they do, they do not have a plan to get there. In a word, they lack direction.

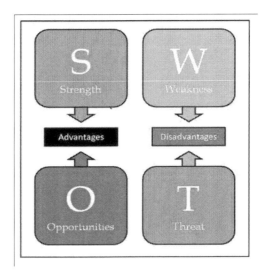

TAKE AWAY ACTIVITY
CHAPTER 3
ASSESSING YOUR ORGANIZATION

List your Strengths and Weaknesses and identify any external Threats
or Opportunities.

SWOT ANALYSIS

Strength	Weakness
Strength	Weakness
Strength	Weakness
Strength	Weakness
Opportunity	Threat
Opportunity	Threat
Opportunity	Threat
Opportunity	Threat

GUIDING PRINCIPLES
CHAPTER 3
ASSESSING YOUR ORGANIZATION

1. Assessing your organization is a critical first step.

2. Assess your resources and improve what you have first before heading off in a new direction.

3. When you assess your company, review everything: financials; management; systems; infrastructure; talk to customers; talk to employees; observe workflow; sit in on meetings.

4. The leadership quality found most often in great companies is the leader who asks, "What can I do to make you (the employee) successful?"

5. Correct alignment in a company occurs when the actions of the managers and the behavior of the employees produce results that are consistent with the values and vision of the leadership.

6. Many title insurance companies (owners, managers, employees) do not know where they are headed and even when they do, they do not have a plan to get there. In a word, they lack direction.

CHAPTER 4

SETTING CLEAR DIRECTION

In Chapter 3, we established that before you start rowing your lifeboat, you have to assess your company's strengths and weaknesses and those of your competition, and then establish direction. In this chapter, we consider several key business concepts that companies have used to help establish or refine their overall direction.

In the 1990s, when we worked with a company, the first thing we did was establish the company's values and vision. Setting vision and values was very popular among consulting groups at the time and among business authors. Cult-like charismatic visionaries led companies like Apple and Microsoft and other companies wanted to copy their formula for success. In our practice today, we discuss vision and values and three additional related concepts that help companies develop a framework for their business direction: business drivers, mission, and goal statements. Which of these tools you use independently, or in some combination, will depend upon the assessment of your needs and resources.

Guiding Principle

> *Business drivers describe what the business wants to attain.*

As the name implies, business drivers are key factors that point or drive a company in a certain direction, contribute to growth and development, and describe what the business wants to attain. Business drivers create a focal point for actions and strategy. For Apple, developing new and innovative products almost every year has been a key business strategy to create sales. In title insurance agencies and with underwriters before 1990, the typical driver was product quality.

Chicago Title made it a point that if the property did not meet its standards, they would not do the deal. When First America and later Fidelity National burst onto the scene, their strategies were entirely different. Each of these companies emphasized market share. First American set as its goal to pass Chicago Title as the market leader. It used every channel to gain market share in key markets. For example, it signed more agents and offered better underwriting splits, it bought big agencies for over market prices, and it used sales tactics with which it was difficult to compete. Looking at all of its actions at the time it would be called market share driven. First American like Fidelity National realized that the title policy was becoming a commodity. Their strategy shifted away from product and focused on actions designed to gain market share.

Chicago Title took a very different tactic. Historically a quality driven company, Chicago started to focus on customers and customer service. Known at that time for turning customers away, in the 1990s, they tried to create a new culture of service within their company.

At this juncture, it might be useful to distinguish between customer focused and customer service. A customer-focused company spends considerable effort to learn about its customers and potential customers and it designs products and services around customer needs. Customer service on the other hand is the mechanical delivery of products and services in an efficient and professional way. Danny Meyer[2] is his book "Setting the Table," gives excellent examples of the difference between great customer service and showing hospitality.

Guiding Principle

> *Customer service is the mechanical delivery of products and services in an efficient and professional way.*

Many of the world's great restaurants, offer five star food and five star service, yet customers will describe the restaurant as uncomfortable or unfriendly. These restaurants are seldom the top pick for best restaurant in consumers' polls. Why? Because in some cases they self-define what the customer should want rather than focus on

---

[2] Danny Myers. Setting the Table: The Transforming Power of Hospitality in Business, New York, Harper Paperbacks, 2008.

what the customer wants. In other examples, the four star restaurant is only interested in the high-end customer, and only delivers its best service to its best customers.

During the 1990s, Chicago Title spent considerable time and money interviewing agents and retail customers trying to learn what customers really wanted. For a time, their offices and employees became very focused on customers and service, but they had a hard time moving beyond the sales strategy of creating relationships.

At the time, production turn time was a measurable result, and it was something on which Chicago Title and the other underwriters could compete. In hindsight the question is should they have made turn time on commitment a competitive variable? Should they have let this strategy set direction? At the time we started working in the title insurance industry, the average turnaround time on a commitment was probably seven to ten days. Certainly, in a rush, the turnaround could be faster. At this time, new computer technology and record scanning collided with the reengineering movement. At Chicago Title, senior managers asked the question "if the work was reengineered using new technology, how fast could we turnaround a commitment order?"

Thus, "Battle Turn Time" began and it is still being fought today. The only problem was the title insurance companies were giving their Realtor clients something they did not need. Once the Realtor had a commitment returned in a day or three days, they were never going to be pleased with seven to ten days. In fact, they would ask for more, eventually for same day commitments.

Guiding Principle

A customer-focused company learns about its customers.

In companies driven by customer focus, new products and services may be suggested by the customer, but the leadership of the company still has to decide if it wants to take the company in that direction. That is, can the company grow and develop by offering the customer what he/she has stated as a specific need or are there other specified needs that would be better choices?

Guiding Principle

> ### *In customer-focused companies new products and services are identified by the customer.*

Here is a list of business drivers that have been identified by title insurance companies to help develop direction and strategy. Which of these factors drives your business?

1. Customer focus
2. Customer service
3. Employees
4. Market share
5. Products
6. Profit
7. Quality
8. Revenue
9. Sales and marketing
10. Technology

Values

Many title insurance companies are driven by the personal and business values held by the owner(s) of the company. If held deeply enough, personal and business values can describe the culture of a company. For example, according to the Walt Disney Company web site, "The Walt Disney Company and its affiliated companies have remained faithful to their commitment to produce unparalleled entertainment experiences based on the rich legacy of quality creative content and exceptional storytelling." Disney's goal is to provide "quality entertainment for every member of the family." According to Disney, "guests, audiences, consumers and shareholders have come to depend on us for quality, creativity, innovation and integrity." Disney expects these values of its employees.

Values represent what your company stands for and what your employees should strive for in their everyday actions. In essence, values strike at the core beliefs owners and leaders have about how their business should operate. If you Google the word "values" you will find value lists that include over three hundred terms going from Abundance to Zeal.

If you narrow your search to business values, you will find a list of more than thirty terms including:

Accountability	Accuracy	Communications
Continuous Improvement	Cooperation (Teamwork)	Creativity
Customer Focused	Customer Satisfaction	Customer Service
Decisiveness	Develop People	Discipline
Empowerment	Fairness	Harmony
Honesty	Innovation	Integrity
Loyalty	Market Share	Orderliness
Timeliness	Profit	Quality
Regularity	Reliability	Resourcefulness
Respect	Responsiveness	Results oriented
Safety	Service to Society	Speed
Standardization	Systemization	Will to Succeed

In working with a title insurance company, we often facilitate a meeting where the company's executives can read from a list of value words and select the words that best describe the values of the company and its owners. The most common value words used by title insurance companies are Honest, Ethical, Quality, Customer Service, Revenue, and Profitable.

Once we have an agreed on list of value words/statements, we conduct a forced ranking where each word is paired with another word and the group decides which word is more important. In the end, we have the company's values in order of importance. In the example below, ethical and quality come before service, income, and profit. This would be typical of the value statements we encountered in the 1990's.

Example of Values for a Title insurance company in 1990

1. Ethical / Honest
2. Quality
3. Customer service
4. Revenue
5. Profitable

In the example that follows, we have two different companies. In Company 1, profit is the number one value; it comes before customer service and quality. In Company 2, customer service and quality are more important than profit. In both companies, employee empowerment is last on the list and is sixth. Generally, a company will have a hard time living (realizing) any more than three or four values. For all practical purposes, we would combine honest and ethical and focus on the first four values for each company.

Company 1	Company 2
1. Profit	Customer Service
2. Customer Service	Quality
3. Quality	Ethical
4. Ethical	Honest
5. Honest	Profit
6. Empowerment	Empowerment

By identifying and rank ordering your company values, you have taken an important step on the road to setting direction. Companies are driven by certain factors and they are guided by values. If a company is going to describe its vision, develop a mission, or set goals, its values have to be understood and brought into alignment with how the company operates.

Guiding Principle

Rank ordering company values is an important step in setting direction.

Take a few minutes and list and rank order your top five company values. For each value, consider whether the value provides direction for employees. In addition, ask yourself if your leadership and management practices are aligned with these values?

1. _____

2. _____

3. _____

4. _____

5. _____

Vision, Mission, and Goals

Vision, mission, and measurable goals are different but related business ideas. Many of the owners we have met are not very visionary, but they have a purpose for being in business, they are driven by a desire to accomplish something. They are in business for a reason. Determining the reason that the owner is in business, his/her purpose in owning a title insurance company is a critical step in setting direction. In Jim Collin's book Built to Last[3], purpose often dictates whether a company will be in business for twenty or one hundred years. Consider these five different reasons given for being in business. Purpose statements like these have all been uttered by our clients and other owners of title insurance companies.

Owner:
A. I want to make a lot of money.
B. I hated working for a corporation. I want to be my own boss.
C. It is all I have ever done; I started working in high school.
D. I want a secure income, perhaps even a family business.
E. I want to prove that I can be more successful than my father.

Owner A is profit driven. He may take everything out of the company and invest little back. He is not building a company to last.

---

[3] Jim Collins and Jerry I. Porras, *Built to Last: Successful Habits of Visionary Companies*, New York, Harper Business Essentials, 1994.

Owner B is an interesting example, because the direction of the company is set by whatever the owner is doing at that moment. The entire company revolves around the owner.

Owner C was included because many owners have only worked in a title insurance company and therefore trapped by their lack of business experience.

Owner D is the opposite of Owner A. He will invest in the company, but the security of his family may come first. He might be quick to get out of the business when times get hard.

Finally, we included comments from a second-generation owner, Owner E. In this case, we have a son or daughter who is trying to live up to a father's success. Perhaps the best observation in a family business is you cannot compete with the past. You have to compete with the company down the street.

In the five examples of purpose statements, it might be easy to establish direction with each of these owners, but vision will likely escape them. Vision is about what a company will look like in five years. What products will it sell? How will it sell? Who will be its customers? Who will be its employees? Having a vision for the future requires a drive, a fire in the belly. Owner A has no long-term vision except making money and perhaps selling the business at the best time. Owner B might be very visionary, but his vision may change at any moment. This may be an owner who never finishes what he starts. Whereas, Owner E could be the most visionary, if we can get him/her focused on the future.

Guiding Principle

Values represent what your company stands for and what your employees should strive for in their everyday actions.

You may have noticed, not for profit companies often have a mission statement rather than a vision statement. Their mission statements are often a written document hanging on a wall explaining why the company is in business, their purpose. Since not for profit companies are by definition not in business to make money (their profit margin is limited by tax law), they have to explain why they are in business in other terms, what are they trying to accomplish, what is their objective or mission? In general, mission statements describe the purpose of a business, not the owner's purpose. Often, a mission statement describes the group it serves and the service it will provide. For example, here is the on-line statement about the Red Cross:

Since its founding in 1881 by visionary leader Clara Barton, the American Red Cross has been the nation's premier emergency response organization. As part of a worldwide movement that offers neutral humanitarian care to the victims of war, the American Red Cross distinguishes itself by also aiding victims of devastating natural disasters. Over the years, the organization has expanded its services, always with the aim of preventing and relieving suffering.

Note how the Red Cross has the goal of preventing and relieving suffering. In addition, that it is part of a worldwide movement offering neutral humanitarian care, and that it is the nation's (United States) premier emergency response organization. These goals, even if labeled "mission," would have been visionary in 1881 and today.

In the best examples, vision, a company's mission statement or its values help describe the character of the company whereas goal statements sharpen the focus to what the company is trying to achieve. In truth, all these terms overlap, but for practical reasons we often choose to focus on developing goals statements, whereas in the past we worked more with companies to create a future vision.

In the 1990s, when we focused on vision with companies, one of the things we found was a title insurance company's vision quickly turned into a marketing campaign or simply a clever slogan. Unfortunately, in many cases, even when the slogan was remembered, the vision statement never took on any life.

In the early 1990s, Chicago Title decided that it needed to change its image and culture. To do so, it hired several of the largest management-consulting firms, including our prior company COBA, Inc. to help change its culture. In 1991, COBA started an initiative called Managing for Excellence (MFE). In MFE, the top managers at Chicago Title and Ticor were brought together for a series of management seminars. The topics of the seminars were leadership, performance management, customer service, market and sales planning, and teambuilding. Following on the success of MFE, we offered a similar program for Chicago Title's top agents called Partners for Excellence, and Chicago Title started an employee initiative called Quest for Excellence. These two initiatives were later combined into programs for new managers and smaller agents.

Unfortunately, when MFE began, rather than set a vision for the company or for the family of companies, it was decided we would focus on the many regions in the company and try to implement the same set of ideas across each region, including: developing a vision for each region and even visions for each of the larger offices. In hindsight, this was a mistaken idea for the company as a whole, because even today, Chicago Title lacks a unifying vision. On the positive side, creating hundreds of vision statements taught us and Chicago Title's managers a great deal about creating and living a vision.

One of the offices at the time that took this message of vision to heart was the Houston Chicago Title Texas office. This office had lost a lot of money in the past, the competition in Houston was fierce, and the office had a new manager, Susan Tempest. Working with her team of employees and managers, Susan not only turned the company around financially, but she created a vision statement that was both clever and it developed cultural legs, meaning it came to life.

Like many offices, Houston started with what seemed to be just another clever slogan, "At Chicago Title in Houston we have The Stronger Commitment." Anyone in the title insurance industry will immediately see the cleverness of this slogan because the commitment is the legal document the title insurance company issues and it is the basis of its policy. In essence, Houston was saying that its commitment to issue a policy was better than any competitor because Chicago Title stood behind it. Ultimately, the local slogan or catch phrase became simply "The Stronger Commitment." This clever play on words was copied and adopted by a number of other offices, who failed to understand the vision that Susan was trying to create.

For Susan Tempest, the vision statement was more than a clever marketing phrase, it described the way she led the office and the way the people in the office conducted their business. In everything they did, they needed to show a stronger commitment! This meant when the rivers flooded in Houston, CT employees were out filling sandbags. It meant in everything the company did in every customer decision, it had to show a stronger commitment. What Susan accomplished in Houston was remarkable. In a year, she turned around one of the poorest performing offices into the most improved. Here is her story.

THE STRONGER COMMITMENT
By Susan F. Tempest

Susan held senior level positions in operations and national initiatives for both Chicago Title and First American.

The Houston Operation looked like one of those houses you see being renovated: the foundation is cracked, the roof is leaking, and the interior needs to be gutted. You wonder why they didn't just tear the house down – there's nothing of value left! In the early 1990's, the only business the Houston Operation had was Company directed and the Company was getting ready to turn that work over to an agent.

Given the situation, many believed the operation should be shut down. Certainly, with no business, no revenue, no profits, no customers, no direction, it would have been easy to justify. However, I was convinced the operation had 'good bones.' There were good people – they were just going in different directions. We needed everyone to be working on a shared vision for the operation. To get us started, we focused on the People, Processes, and Profits.

People. To achieve success, we needed employees to be emotionally invested. We created **The Stronger Commitment** slogan to get people's attention.. However, we quickly learned that it was an empty statement; it sounded good but it did not translate into a vision. Employees did not understand how they were a part of it. With input from the employees, we expanded the slogan into the following vision:

THE STRONGER COMMITMENT transforms promises into reality. It represents actions that speak louder than words. Commitment is the base we draw on when we are out of patience, understanding, and energy. It is taking time when there is none.

THE STRONGER COMMITMENT is what binds us to each other, to our customers, and to a level of service that goes beyond what is expected. It means believing in your contribution to the overall goal and in the power that you possess to make a difference every day. Commitment is the essence of character and integrity.

The Houston Operation has THE STRONGER COMMITMENT to building a service culture which provides a Commitment to Insuring Customer Success through empowering employees and listening to customers.

Our vision statement became the cornerstone to everything we did. The entire operation signed off on **The Stronger Commitment** and we delivered it (with everyone's signatures) to prospective customers and potential employees.

Once our vision was communicated, we set goals with specific strategies so we would know when we achieved **The Stronger Commitment**. Our goals included:

1. Triple market share in three years.
    a. We needed customers.
    b. We needed traction in the market place. Slogans, mission statements, visions, goals – they are all worthless unless you have customers.
2. Invest in people internally and externally.
    a. Align employees' goals with the operation and review their performance twice a year. Completing reviews was factored into managers' incentives.
    b. Interview customers and respond with proposals that incorporated their input. Then deliver the service.
    c. People who thought they were indispensable to the operation threatened to leave – we took them up on their offer. They had a different agenda and it would be best for the employees and the customers to have one vision.

Process. From our interviews, we learned that customers were frustrated because they could not get through to their escrow officers. Instead of hiring more staff, we reviewed what the escrow officer was doing. We determined that if the process did not touch the customer, it should be either migrated to a centralized source, automated, or eliminated. Lesson learned: Make sure the people touching the customer are doing what is most important to the customer.

All employees were encouraged to submit ideas for process improvement. Managers had annual goals of implementing the approved ideas. Lesson Learned: After employees get over the shock of changing processes, they become addicted to it. They start expecting and demanding more and more improvements. Status quo is a letdown.

Profits. Financials were reviewed with the same level of scrutiny as processes. What were we spending money on and how was that valuable to the customer? Employees were responsible for bringing in business and servicing it. Management was charged with managing the expenses so we could realize sustained profitability. Profitability was expected.

By explaining how the employee contributes to the operations and customer's success, by listening to the customer, by changing processes to support customers' needs, and by communicating progress, the Houston Operation became The Stronger Commitment.

Accomplishing a vision can only happen if the leader is the visionary and the vision becomes the culture. One of the reasons we have focused less on talking about visions and more about goal statements is the idea that goals are simpler. Visions are dreams, goals are a reality, and they can be expressed in terms that are measurable. For example, "We want to be number one in market share," or "We want to have the best commercial closing unit in the city." When we ask a non-visionary owner where is the company headed, he\she will talk about the size of the company, the number of offices, the number of employees, the level of income or profit. These are ideas that are less lofty than vision, and therefore easier for employees to understand and easier to measure and assess.

Guiding Principle

> *Accomplishing a vision can only happen if the leader is visionary and the vision becomes the culture.*

We once worked with a hospital that had hired a well-known accounting/consulting company to develop the hospital's new vision. The process took over a year, cost over a quarter of a million dollars, and produced a three hundred plus page document describing the vision and values of the hospital, based around ten "we will be," vision statements that the president of the hospital had laminated on desk plaques for all the managers and doctors. A year later, we were hired to help the hospital bring the vision to life. For months, we tried to convince the president and vice presidents of the hospital that no one could remember ten vision statements and the hospital needed to simplify its vision. Finally, the issue came to a head when the president held a management meeting to discuss the vision and he could not remember all ten statements.

For us, rather than try to finely craft a vision statement, we would rather focus on where a company is headed by setting measurable goals. Having said that goal setting is easier, we do not want a leader with vision to give up the idea of crafting a vision. Often times where we are trying to engineer, production workflow, we will ask the owner or the manager how he/she envisions the change.

One time, working in the same hospital, we sat in a design session where the director of pediatric care described what she envisioned in their new nighttime pediatric center. To paraphrase her, she said *imagine a mother walking into the center at 2:30 a.m. She has three children with her, one a baby in her arms. The baby has been up all night crying and coughing. The mother has not slept and is frantic. On entering the facility, the mother is met by a nurse and taken directly into an observation room. Using a wireless computer tablet, the nurse establishes names and who is the patient. Knowing that the mother needs relief and the ability to focus, the nurse calls an aid to watch the children while the baby is examined by a doctor who has entered the room. In less than fifteen minutes the baby is diagnosed and being treated. Once the treatment is established, the family is moved to an area where medical information is taken and the billing procedures are explained.*

When you contrast this idea to what most of us have experienced in a hospital emergency room, you can see what we mean when we say vision and values describes how a company will look and feel. Having a vision and living a vision are possible but it requires leadership and complete commitment at the very top of the organization, and it takes a nearly cult like culture dedicated to living the vision. Short of these components, a company is better off starting by developing measurable goals.

In our organizational assessment, we said that we establish direction by asking the owners about short and long-term goals. Generally, their goals will include:

1. Market share / residential and commercial
2. Gross income
3. Total expenses
4. Labor expenses
5. Profit
6. Profit margin
7. Operational performance
8. Number of offices
9. Use of technology
10. Reputation as a title insurance company
11. Reputation as an employer
12. Position in the community

Clearly, these twelve dimensions are related, but it is important to understand that some owners have revenue goals but do not care about market share. Likewise an owner can have a profit goal, without concern for the margin, meaning he wants $300,000 profit however the company can get it. Because we have worked with some of the top title agents in the country, many of the owners we have worked with are concerned about being the best or number one in their market.

Being Number One in a market of course could mean being number one in market share, but often market share in the title insurance industry can be measured by orders, closings, or revenue. Often times a company will be recognized by the top customers as the best company, but not have the highest number of orders or dollars.

For example, we worked with a company in New Mexico, that prided itself on being number one in commercial, which it was, but it was not even in the top three in residential closings. When the owner interviewed customers, he was shocked to realize that what made him tops in commercial was a reputation for being exact and being thorough, which translated to difficult and slow for residential realtors.

By interviewing potential realtor customers, the owner realized if he wanted to be tops in residential he would need a different team of title and escrow staff or they would need to produce residential orders differently. In this company, the values and culture that made them the best in commercial were misaligned with being the best in residential. If the owner wanted to be the top residential title insurance company and the top commercial company, he was going to have to change his reputation and he was going to have to change his operational performance. Setting practical (concrete) goals help to focus on measurable results and tactics for change.

Guiding Principle

> *If a company is not capable of developing a visionary culture, it is better off focusing on achieving measurable goals.*

In the simplest case, when we establish the direction of a company, we are setting revenue and profit goals for the year and we are establishing whether there are any sales or operational initiatives that require planning. For example, if the owner plans to open a new office, there are a number of critical events that will require leadership and management (planning). If the company has more than one office, part of setting direction means setting goals for the offices.

Before leaving the topic of setting goals, it is important to understand that the goals have to pass the BASIC test.

Believable
Achievable
Stretch
In **C**ontrol

In setting goals, it is critical that the people who are responsible for achieving the goal have the power, authority, and skills necessary to achieve the goal. Collectively, we say the person or people responsible have to be In Control.

Guiding Principle

Goals have to pass the BASIC Test.

A number is not a goal unless it has stretch. For example, if a company has averaged 50 orders a month for five years in a row, there is no point setting the goal at 50 again, unless the market has dropped so much that achieving 50 again will be difficult. Generally, goals should push us to improve by 5, 10, or even 15 percent. Goals that ask for 25 percent improvement or growth are harder and represent a significant or strategic level of change. Setting this much stretch requires the goal to pass the laugh test, meaning no one thinks the goal is a joke, either too easy or too difficult.

Even when people believe they can achieve a goal, some goals will not pass the Achievable Test. Sometimes a group can be convinced that it can achieve a goal when in fact, history or reality says otherwise. For example, when we were first teaching managers to set sales goals, they might set a goal of 50% increase in sales when they had never experienced even a 5% growth. With learning and experience, they came to set goals that had a stretch of a 10% increase in sales but were also believable.

Beyond setting financial, operational, and sales goals, you should include any Human Resource, Information Technology, or staff developmental goals or initiatives for the year. For example, installing a new order tracking system or offering management training to the new managers. Finally, in setting goals, you want to make sure that any personal goals for the owners are made clear.

TAKE AWAY ACTIVITY
CHAPTER 4
SETTING CLEAR DIRECTION

1. Using our list of values, identify 3 to 5 values that are critical to your company. Write a statement explaining what the value is and why each value is important.

2. Write a statement that explains where your company is headed. What is its purpose? What is your vision for the company? If possible, complete this with a group of managers.

3. Write measurable goals for your company in the following categories:

GOALS

Gross Income:
Open Orders:
Labor Expense:
Profit:
Title Operations:
Escrow Operations:
Other Operations:
Sales:

GUIDING PRINCIPLES
CHAPTER 4
SETTING CLEAR DIRECTION

1. Business drivers are key factors that point or drive a company in a certain direction, contribute to growth and development, and describe what the business wants to attain.

2. A customer-focused company spends considerable effort to learn about its customers and potential customers and it designs products and services around those needs.

3. Customer service is the mechanical delivery of products and services in an efficient and professional way.

4. In companies driven by customer focus, new products and services may be suggested by the customer, but the leadership of the company still has to decide if it wants to take the company in that direction.

5. Values represent what your company stands for and what your employees should strive for in their everyday actions.

6. By identifying and rank ordering your company values, you have taken an important first step on the road to setting direction.

7. Accomplishing a vision can only happen if the leader is visionary and the vision becomes the culture.

8. If a company is not capable of developing a visionary culture, it is better starting by developing measurable goals.

9. Goals have to pass the BASIC Test: Believable, Achievable, Stretch, and In Control.

CHAPTER 5

MEASURES AND METRICS

In every business, there are important bits of information, data that should be recorded and reported. Obviously, for tax purposes, a business has to keep track of certain critical pieces of information, for example, revenue and expenses, profit and losses. If the IRS did not require a business to report this information, some businesses would never measure and keep track of their own performance. In the past when we would request financials from a title insurance company, the owner would have to call his/her accountant and days later, we would get a year old report. Today, most businesses measure their financial and operational performance on a daily basis, and keep track of far more than revenue and expense.

In Chapter 5, we examine critical measures and metrics for use in managing and leading a title insurance company. To start, we examine the five basic measures of any title insurance company and then we explore metrics that can be used to project trends and predict future performance. In every title insurance company, there are five operational measures we like to track and five financial measures:

Financial
1. Gross Revenue
2. Indirect Expenses (Cost of Sales)
3. Operating Income
4. Direct Expenses (Operating Expenses)
5. Profit

Operational
1. Orders received
2. Policies issued
3. Closings
4. Closed (paid) orders
5. Number of Full Time Employees (FTE)

Title Insurance Company Measures

In a title insurance company, Gross Revenue is income derived from all sources. Gross Income includes revenue from paid orders, closing revenue, money collected for fees, income from title services, and income from interest on corporate savings. In managing a business, we have to make a distinction between gross income and operating income. Operating Income is the money that remains in a company's bank account after it pays out indirect expenses, expenses associated with underwriting and other cost of sales. For example, if you have to hire an outside closer or pay for an out of county title search, these expenses are considered a Cost of Sales or an indirect expense. Fees paid to record documents or transfer documents; fees associated with a settlement or closing are all Cost of Sales and have to subtract from gross revenue. Essentially, this income, which can be 15-30% of your gross income, is money you have to pay out before you run your business, therefore it should not be treated as operating income.

Operating income is the money that you can use to run your company and pay your direct expenses. In most title insurance companies, the operating income is approximately 80% -70% of gross income. In manufacturing businesses, operating income can be as little as 25% of gross income. In states where the underwriting split is regulated, for example Texas, the percent of gross revenue going to Cost of Sales (CoS) should be fairly stable, and therefore understandable or predictable. For example, if you had gross revenues of five million and 20% of your gross goes to CoS, then your operating income is four million.

Gross Revenue	=	$5,000,000.00	100%
Cost of Sales	=	$1,000,000.00	20%
Operating Income	=	$4,000.000.00	80%

In budget planning, it is important for a manager to understand his/her operating income as a percent of gross income. In this example, if the company's direct or operating expenses are less than four million, the company makes money. If the direct expenses are more than four million, the company loses money.

If you know that your operating income is 80% of your gross revenue, then you can determine how much gross revenue you will need at any level of direct expense. For example, suppose this year we want to hire several new staff and we estimate that our operating expenses will be $4,890,000. Using simple math, we know that our gross revenue will have to be $4,890,000 /.80 = $6,112,500 just to break even.

In many companies, the operating income is determined after Cost of Sales is subtracted and after administration costs or other operating fees are assessed. For example, in a company with ten offices and a central title plant, each office is assessed an administration fee and a title plant fee. Typically, administration and title plant fees are charged back to an office as a percentage of gross revenue or they are charged for each person and each order in an office. For example, if the company in the example above assessed a 10% administration fee and a 10% title fee, the operating income would be 60% of gross revenue or three million. In planning to manage a branch operation knowing that you can only operate on 60% of your gross is a critical metric.

Measure	Actual	Percent of Gross
Gross Revenue	+ $5,000,000.00	100%
Cost of Sales	- $1,000,000.00	20%
Administration	- $ 5000,000.00	10%
Title fee	- $ 5000,000.00	10%
Operating Income	= $3,000.000.00	60%

Once we understand our gross revenue, our indirect expenses, and our operating income, we have to consider our direct expenses. The single largest expense category in any title insurance company is wages and salaries. Collectively, wages, salaries, bonus, retirement, employee taxes, and employee benefits make up the budget category called Labor Expense. In managing the finances of a business, there are two ratios related to Labor Expense that are important to understand. The first is your Labor Expense to Total Expense Ratio, or Labor to Expense ratio (LTE).

Labor Ratio

In professional companies, like doctor practices and law firms, labor expense can be more than 50% of the total expense. In manufacturing companies and companies with a heavy investment in brick and mortar or technology, labor expense can be less than 25% of the total expense, i.e., a Labor to Expense ratio less than .25. In title insurance companies, providing good service typically requires people, therefore, labor expense can be as much or more than 50% of the total expenses. However, when labor expense becomes too high (over .70), it usually means there are a few highly paid employees. In terms of staffing for profit, since labor is the single biggest expense, what you are spending on labor relative to revenue, becomes a critical ratio.

For our purpose, Labor Ratio expresses labor expense as a percentage of total revenue (L/R). In terms of staffing for profit, Labor Ratio is the single most important factor in determining the health and profit of a title insurance company. In our experience, even in good times when the ratio of Labor to Revenue (i.e., Labor Expense / Gross Revenue) exceeds .50, a title insurance company will have unacceptable profit levels. In some areas of the country, this ratio will have to be significantly below .50 for a company to be profitable because their other fixed expenses are high.

Guiding Principle

> **Labor Ratio is the most important factor in determining the health and profit of a title insurance company.**

When the market has been down for a long period, it is likely that a title insurance company will reduce staff and therefore lower its labor ratio. Unfortunately, some companies are slow to react and some never cut enough, meaning that those companies that reduced staff may be more profitable and more competitive. In some cases, we have seen labor levels less than 25% of revenue, however, at some point a reduction in staff (i.e., labor ratio) will cause products and customer service to suffer, so the lowest ratio possible for a title business is a question best left to what employee levels will maintain service.

Determining a proper level of staffing in order to ensure both profit and good service is a complicated question. The problem for a small company is predicting orders and revenue in an uncertain future. Without a good measure of future revenue, it is nearly impossible to determine how large a reduction or increase you need to make in your staff. The question for companies today is whether your labor ratio is sufficiently low enough to be profitable.

If you are currently operating at a loss or just breaking even, it most likely means that your labor is still too high. Determining the proper level of staff in order to make a profit is not complicated at one level. It is a mathematical question and only requires the necessary financial and performance data, and the right metric. What is difficult is determining which people to keep and whether you have the right people for the future.

Guiding Principle

> ### *If you are currently operating at a loss or breaking even, your labor is too high.*

So far, we have discussed Labor Ratio as a metric that can be used to determine the likelihood that a title insurance company will be profitable. The difficulty with using Labor Ratio for managing a business is that it is a trailing measure, meaning that it is determined after the orders are closed, employees are paid, and the work is done. Long term, Labor Ratio is an excellent metric, but you need a leading measure you can look at daily or weekly.

In title insurance companies, we use a simple, easy to understand metric that relates revenue to labor expense like Labor Ratio, but one that can be measured earlier in the business cycle. For most companies, determining what a company will spend on wages and salary is easier than determining all labor expense, i.e., including incentives and benefits. For that reason, for the remainder of the chapter, we will use "salaries" to mean all wages and salaries and we will refer to salaries as a substitute for total labor cost.

Likewise, orders is a simple leading measure that can be used as a substitute for revenue. Orders can be easily counted and tracked and they come in a month or two before revenue. Closings or actual paid orders are measures that may seem like a more reliable substitute for revenue because they have a higher correlation with revenue, but they are not leading measures. We like orders because with a little simple math you can easily determine how many orders are needed to break even and how many orders are needed to make any profit goal.

For example, consider a company that received 1,200 orders (100 per month) last year and had gross revenues of $1,200,000 and $1,000,000 in total expenses. Using these statistics, we determine the average income per order. In this example, $1,000.00 per order. Based on this information, this year for planning purposes, we now know we need at least 84 orders a month to break even if nothing changes.

In planning, you should pick the measure that best represents your mix of income and the measure for which you have the most data. In our example, we will use new open orders each month. Using orders as a substitute for revenue has some obvious problems. One problem is that not all orders turn into closings or paid orders. A second problem is the revenue on different types of orders can vary considerably.

If you use open orders as your metric for future revenue you may want to determine your capture rate or fallout rate. For example, for every 100 open orders, 80 orders end up closing or being paid, i.e., an 80% capture rate. In the example above, we earn $1,000 on 1,200 open orders. However, our income per paid order is $1,200.

In companies with a large commercial presence, you may need to classify orders by type, for example, residential versus commercial orders, because your average income from these different types of orders can be significantly different.

We started out this section by stating that Labor was the single biggest expense in a title insurance company and we stated that one of the critical metrics for a title insurance company is the Labor to Revenue ratio. We also stated that Labor Ratio is a trailing measure. For this discussion, we are going to use the ratio of Orders to Employees as a leading metric because it is easy to determine every day. In title insurance companies, we measure Orders to Employees by dividing open orders by the number of full time employees. For example, if a company has 10 full time employees and opened 100 orders in a month, we could say their Orders to Employee ratio was 10 orders per 1 person per month or 10 to 1. In addition, we know this company needs to take in 8.4 orders per person to break even.

Guiding Principle

> *Labor ratio is a trailing measure.*
>
> *You need a leading measure.*

Order to FTE

In this metric, Orders is a substitute for revenue and Employee is a substitute or short hand measure for salaries. In using this metric, we assume that the average salary is representative of the majority of your workforce. One complication with using the number of employees or head count as a substitute for Labor Expense is Labor expense can vary significantly based on the number of days in the month, the number of hours that each employee worked, and the number of overtime hours paid in a month. In order to take into account the days in the month, paid hours and overtime, we calculate a number called Full Time Employees or Full Time Equivalent (FTE). To determine your total FTE's you divide the total number of paid hours you have in a period by the regular paid hours in the period for one full time employee.

Table 1 shows how to determine FTE. In this example taken from a title insurance company in the month of August of 2008, there were 21 working days in August and the company had eight employees who were paid hourly and seven employees who received a salary. In total, with overtime, the company paid the equivalent of 16.25 full time employees. In other words, the company paid for the equivalent of one and a quarter extra persons (1.25 FTE) in the month of August. For this company, simply eliminating overtime hours and finding a way to get the work accomplished during normal working hours would eliminate the expense equivalent of one and a quarter persons, thereby improving the labor ratio and making the company more productive.

In order to calculate FTE for a company, you have to include all the employees in the company, regardless of their contribution to revenue or orders and closings. This means counting sales, admin staff, managers, and executives. In companies with a small number of full time employees and no overtime, head count can be used instead of calculating FTE. Because we are using FTE as our substitute measure for salaries, our metric now becomes Orders to FTE.

Guiding Principle

> ***Open Orders to Full Time Equivalents is a leading metric.***

Establishing Orders to FTE standards or goals for your business may make all the difference in your business. To start, we recommend establishing an Orders to FTE standard for your company as a whole and then creating separate title and escrow standards. By standard, we mean the level you need to have to meet your profit goals. Your Orders to FTE standard represents the level below which you do not want to go in any given month.

Table 1. Determining FTE

Work Days. Number of days in the period.	221
Hours in a Day. Number of paid hours in a regular workday.	18
Hours in a Month. Calculate the regular paid hours in the period for one full time employee. In this example (21 * 8 =168)	1168
Paid Hours in a Month. Determine the number of regular hours actually paid for all hourly employees, including all paid time off (PTO), i.e., vacation, sick, holidays, in the time period	11344
Paid Salary Hours in a Month. Determine the number of hours paid in time period for salaried employees	11176
Overtime. Determine the number of overtime hours paid in the period, in this example, 140. Multiply the overtime hours by 1.5. In this example 140*1.5 = 210	2210
Total Hours paid in a Month. Add the total paid hours for hourly employee, salaried employees plus overtime. In this example, 1344 + 1176+210 = 2730	22730
Full Time Employees. Divide the total paid hours by the regular paid hours for one employee in the period. In this example, 2730 ÷168 = 16.25.	116.25

Returning to our example, the company paid for 16.25 FTE in August of 2008. That year, the company opened 225 orders in August. Using our Orders to FTE formula, the company's Orders to FTE ratio for August would be 13.85 open orders per FTE per month (i.e., 225/16.25 = 13.85), meaning 13.85 open orders per FTE per month for the 21 working days in August, or .66 open orders per FTE per day.

At this point, it is important to ask, 'How good is a result of 13.85 open orders per FTE per month?' The reason a simple statistic like Orders to FTE is useful is because orders are a substitute for revenue and FTE is a substitute for salaries. For example, if we know that the average income from an order is $1,000.00, and that the average pay for an employee is $3,000.00 a month, then we know that we need at least 3 orders per person just to cover our labor cost. Likewise, if labor is 40% of our expenses, then we know we need more than eight open orders per month per person before we have a dollar of profit.

Armed with this knowledge we can set a goal for a company's Order to FTE ratio that should keep the company in the black. Naturally, the number for your operation will be different from our example. It may even be different from the number for the company down the street, because each title insurance company operates under different conditions, markets and regulations and has different structures designed for their operations to deliver their products and services. The number for your company has to take your particular situation into account, the revenue from an order, the cost of an employee, etc.

To help you set your own standard or goal for Orders to FTE, we have developed a simple six-step process. In explaining the model, we will use a number of terms that have proven to be useful in our consulting. Because this is a financial or budgeting model, we want to start with an adequate amount of financial data, six to twelve months at a minimum.

The order in which you complete these steps is not critical; rather having a reliable set of data that reflects your current financial condition is what is important.

1. Determine your total open orders in a year.
2. Determine your total revenue from orders for the year.
3. Determine your total expenses before profit distribution.
4. Determine what you spend on total salaries annually.
5. Determine how many FTEs or paid hours you had in a year.
6. Determine your profit or loss for the year.

Using these six pieces of data, there are eight calculations that you will need to perform on the information. Once the calculations are completed, you can put together a simple table or spreadsheet to determine your current Orders to FTE ratio and use that number to set a standard or goal for the future.

1. Average open orders per month.
2. Average income per order (Total Revenue / Total Orders).
3. Average FTEs per month.
4. Average Total Expenses per month (Total Expense / the number of months in the period).
5. Average salaries expense per month, (Total Salaries / the number of months in the period).
6. Average Expenses Other Than Salary (OTS) each month, (Expense – Salaries = OTS).
7. Average Salary per FTE (Salaries / FTE).
8. Calculate the percentage salaries represents of your total expenses. (Salaries/Total Expense). This is your Salaries to expense ratio.

In Table 2, we show an example where a company breaks even when they take in 10.91 orders per person per month, or 150 total orders with 13.75 FTE. It should be noted that this example was created simply to show the mechanics of calculating Orders to FTE. In our example, the company averages $500.0 on an order, a value that is probably below your average. Based on this information, the company makes no profit when the Orders to FTE ratio is 10 to 1. Considering the numbers, in this example, the question is, at what point does the company make money?

In Table 3, the company makes a little over 10% profit (the industry average) when orders increase from 150 to 172 per month. This increase in orders results in 12.51 orders per person and lowers Salaries to Revenue to 39% of Total Revenue.

In Table 4, the same level of profit also could have been obtained at the original level 150 orders, if the level of staffing (FTE) had decreased to 10.5 FTE per month. Reducing staff by 3.25 FTE not only improves profit and profit margin, but it improves both the Orders to FTE Ratio to 14 to 1 and lowers the Salaries to Revenue to 34 percent.

In setting a standard for your business, you have to determine your breakeven point and the level of profit and profit margin that you desire. Measuring Orders per FTE (OFTE) by the method presented will provide you with a simple way for evaluating staffing levels based on trends in monthly orders. If you know that fewer orders are coming through the door then you can take steps to improve your Orders per FTE ratio before your profit suffers. Determining Orders per FTE on a monthly basis gives you a metric to judge your level of staffing and it provides a way to think about changes in staffing when orders start to decrease or increase.

Table 2. Example of measures when a company breaks even.

Measure	Calculation	Result
Monthly Revenue from Orders	From P&L or calculated	$75,000
Average Income per Open Order	Revenue / Orders	$500
Average Open Orders per month	Total Open Orders / months	150
Cost of Sales (e.g., Underwriting)	From P&L or calculated	$15,000
Salary Expense	From P&L or calculated	$33,750
Other than Salary Expenses	From P&L or calculated	$26,250
Estimated Total Expenses	From P&L or calculated	$75,000
Average Total FTEs per month	From Payroll	13.75
Average Salary per FTE	Salaries / FTEs	$2,454.55
Open Orders to FTE	Open Orders / FTEs	10.91
Salaries to Gross Revenue	Total salaries / Gross Revenue	45%
Salaries to Total Expense	Salaries / Total Expenses	45%
Estimated Profit	Revenue - Expenses	$0.00
Profit per Order	Profit / Orders	$0.00
Profit Margin	Profit / Revenue	0.00%

Table 3. The Company is profitable by lowering labor cost.

Metric	Calculation	Result
Average Open Orders per month	Total Open Orders / months	172
Average Total FTEs per month	From Payroll	13.75
Open Orders to FTE	Open Orders / FTEs	12.51
Estimated Profit	Revenue – Expenses	$8,400
Salaries to Gross Revenue	Total salaries / Gross Revenue	39.24%
Salaries to Expense	Salaries / Total Expenses	43.72%
Profit per Order	Profit / Orders	$51.16
Profit Margin	Profit / Revenue	10.23%

Table 4. The Company is profitable by improving orders to FTE.

Metric	Calculation	Result
Average Open Orders per month	Total Open Orders / months	150
Average Total FTEs per month	From Payroll	10.50
Open Orders to FTE	Open Orders / FTEs	14.29
Estimated Profit	Revenue – Expenses	$7,977.33
Salaries to Gross Revenue	Total salaries / Gross Revenue	34.36%
Salaries to Expense	Salaries / Total Expenses	38.45%
Profit per Order	Profit / Orders	$53.18
Profit Margin	Profit / Revenue	10.64%

TAKE AWAY ACTIVITY
CHAPTER 5
MEASURES AND METRICS

1. Select a period for which you have reliable data, e.g., 6 months. Determine the number for each item on the table below during that period. Based on these numbers, you can begin to manage by the numbers.

	Open orders
	Total revenue from orders
	Total expenses
	Total labor
	FTEs
	Profit or loss
	Labor / Revenue
	Revenue / Orders
	Expenses / (Revenue / Orders)
	Orders to FTE

GUIDING PRINCIPLES
CHAPTER 5
MEASURES AND METRICS

1. Labor Ratio (i.e., labor expense / gross revenue) is the single most important factor in determining the health and profit of a title insurance company.

2. If you are currently operating at a loss or just breaking even, it most likely means that your labor is still too high.

3. For the longer term, Labor Ratio is an excellent metric, it is what we call a trailing measure because it is determined after orders are closed, employees are paid and the work is done. You also need a leading measure you can look at every day.

4. Acting as a substitute for the ratio of revenue to salaries, the ratio of open orders to employees or Full Time Equivalents (FTE's) is a leading metric that you can determine each day, week and monthly.

5. Establish an Order to FTE standard for your company as a whole and separate FTE title and escrow standards. By standard, we mean the level you need to meet your profit goals. Your Orders to FTE (OFTE) standard represents the level below which you do not want to go in any given month.

6. Determining Orders per FTE on a monthly basis gives you a metric to judge your level of staffing and it provides a way to think about changes in staffing when orders start to decrease or increase.

MANAGEMENT

CHAPTER 6

DEVELOPING YOUR TEAM

A title insurance company is a system of interrelated functions and components that includes groups of people who work together in various types of teams. The work flows from one person to the next in these teams and then is passed on to another team to complete another phase of the work. For example, the work starts with a team of people who do order entry and then the work flows to the title and escrow production teams. Other types of teams in title insurance companies include management, administration, and sales. In order for the company to be successful, the teams have to function effectively as units and with the other teams.

Guiding Principle

Teamwork results in greater productivity and better service.

What makes some teams successful and others not? Every team is a group of people, but not every group of people is a team. A team is a special kind of group that is defined in terms of its goals and how it goes about achieving them. A team must have goals that can be achieved only through the cooperation and combined efforts of all of its members. In the title insurance industry, teamwork can lead to consistent approaches to customers, increased responsibility and ownership for products and services, and improvements in morale. In the end, the value of teamwork in a title insurance company is that it results in greater productivity and better service.

In Chapter 6 we focus on developing management and work teams. You will find information about team structure and processes and using teams in a title insurance company. From an owner's perspective, management team development should focus on determining whether the right people have been correctly slotted to fill key executive and management positions and whether the correct management structure and processes are in place.

An owner can start at the very top of the company and assess whether the right people have been chosen for key positions. Unfortunately, we have known many owners who have struggled with the placement of the wrong people in key executive and management positions. In some cases, managers have been left in positions long past the time they should have been replaced. One important way to evaluate whether managers have the correct skills and abilities to function successfully is to evaluate their behavior in the context of good management team structure and processes.

Management Teams

Several years ago, we started working with a title insurance agency whose owner had all twelve of the title and escrow office managers of the company, and a sales manager, reporting to her. The owner had a financial person that helped with the books and billing, but no other executive staff. The owner made sure she had a hand in all the operational decisions that needed to be made each day. The owner complained she never had time to do anything except answer questions and take care of problems the managers should be handling.

The managers complained it was not clear what they were responsible for achieving. The managers and their employees also complained about confusing lines of authority and poor communication. When there was a major problem in operations, the owner would often rush in and handle the situation with the employee in question or with a customer. As a group, the managers met very infrequently throughout the year and there was little sharing of information or joint problem solving and planning. We quickly discovered there were several recommendations we could make to improve the management structure and the overall functioning of the management team. We also knew with a new structure and processes in place, the owner would have a much better vantage point to evaluate her key management personnel.

In the months that followed, we worked with the owner and her managers to build and develop the following management team structure and processes around seven key areas.

1. Organizational chart
2. Expectations
3. Job Descriptions
4. Goals
5. Team Meetings
6. Communication
7. Evaluative feedback

Organizational chart. One of the first questions we asked the owner is whether she had an organizational chart that depicted reporting relationships among the managers and employees of the company. She quickly showed us an impressive looking chart that clearly outlined the reporting relationships and lines of authority for all the managers. However, once we interviewed the managers we learned what the organizational chart showed on paper was very different from what was functionally occurring with her and the managers. The owner had all of the managers of the company reporting to her and, we knew it was too many for her to accomplish everything she needed to do as an owner. Much of the time she should have been devoting to oversight, financial and strategic planning and customer development was being diverted to tasks the managers should have been handling themselves. We recommended that the new management structure includes a chief operations officer (COO) position that would relieve her of directly working with all the managers on a daily basis.

Title companies vary widely in terms of size, make-up and scope of operations and what makes sense for some large companies in terms of management structure may not be called for in smaller companies. Larger title insurance companies, at the executive level, should consider having an executive team consisting of, in addition to the owner or Chief Executive Officer, a Chief Financial Officer (CFO), a Chief Operations Officer (COO), an executive in charge of sales, a Human Resources Director, and an Information Technology Officer (ITO). Smaller companies can combine executive functions and work with fewer personnel.

The organizational chart the owner shared with us also did not show that the management group was not learning from and assisting each other, there was no brainstorming and problem solving among the group, and creative energy and enthusiasm were missing. In short, the management team was not functioning like a team at all and the owner

91

was not relying on them for any type of supportive assistance. Moreover, although the lines on the chart showed clear lines of authority and responsibility, in reality, the managers were un-clear on what was expected of them.

Expectations. We knew that setting expectations for the team would be an important way to communicate and define the specific behavior managers should exhibit as team members. The management team expectations we developed included the behavior expected at team meetings as well as the types of ongoing interaction among team member expected on a daily basis. For example, we recommended managers at team meetings report on operational results, provide creative input and ideas, provide feedback on employee behavior and issues, report on customer issues, assist with operational issues, and, contribute to the company planning process.

Guiding Principle

> *Set clear expectations for your management team members.*

On a daily basis, we recommended management team members should be expected to: communicate with fellow team members when needed, assist with problems when called upon by other managers, proactively alert team members to potential file problems both upstream and downstream in the production workflow, and share important customer information.

Job descriptions. Job descriptions that detail responsibilities are a common Human Resource (HR) function and managers in title insurance companies should have them. They did not exist for the title insurance company in our example and we recommended that they be developed to include a strong emphasis on team development and participation.

Goals. Managers should have yearly goals that are set with them by their supervisor. Goals should include financial and operational performance, individual professional development, and, goals that focus on team development and interaction, including work with the management team.

Guiding Principle

> **Managers should have written job descriptions, responsibilities, and goals that include team development and participation.**

Team meetings. We recommended that the management team meets at least quarterly and as necessary. The meetings would follow a standard agenda that was developed and distributed ahead of the meeting. The meetings would be facilitated by the owner, or the soon to be appointed COO, who would keep the team on task and adhere to a set time limit. We recommend not more than 90 minutes to 2 hours for regularly scheduled meetings.

The power of a team in part is what the group can accomplish together and the assistance the group can lend to each other. Our challenge was to instill this idea with both the owner and her managers. Team meetings create the opportunity for both learning and development. Over time we knew this management team could successfully develop and grow to routinely accomplish a number of varied tasks including reviewing operational results, solving company issues, developing new operational procedures, critiquing new programs and initiatives, helping plan new strategy, and, providing important feedback and insight to the owner and the executive team.

Guiding Principle

> **The power of a team is what the group can accomplish as a whole and the assistance they can lend each other.**

Communication. Ongoing and frequent communication is an important process for successful management teams. In addition to the management team meeting regularly, we recommended that management team members: conduct meetings with their own staff monthly, hold face-to-face meetings with individual staff when necessary, hold informal "huddles" daily with staff to discuss immediate production and customer issues, and, use email communications. We also added this word of warning: emails cannot adequately replace face-to-face contact for many situations and managers should be judicious in their use and not over-rely on them.

Evaluative feedback. Providing evaluative feedback for manager behavior and performance is also an important process to build into the development of your management team. We recommend that managers receive evaluative feedback frequently at least quarterly.

Guiding Principle

Provide frequent communications and evaluative feedback for manager behavior and performance.

Work Teams

Whether we are talking about a successful sports franchise or different types of work and office teams in a title insurance company, there are several actions managers and leaders can take to develop, support and reinforce superior teamwork and success. If you are a leader or manager of work or office teams, here are a number of questions that can be asked to assess what actions need to be taken for team development.

Teamwork Questions

1. Do you or your managers know how to develop a team?
2. Do your work teams need to improve in terms of ability, productivity, quality, or cost?
3. Do your teams maximize the potential of individual team members?
4. Do your teams work effectively with other teams in the company?
5. Do your customers receive the needed levels of service and quality?
6. Are team goals or purpose clear for all teams?
7. Are employees positive about their work and work levels?
8. Are team cooperating or supporting each other?
9. Are individuals willing to take on responsibilities?
10. Do individuals take initiative?
11. Do you hear "How can I help?"
12. Do the teams work independently?

If you answered "No" to a majority of questions, you have team problems. In general, successful teams and team members have great technical skills (i.e., they know how to do their work and work effectively). However, beyond individual success, successful teams combine their individual work and work effectively as a group. In other words, they are an effective team. Think of your favorite sports team. Chances are the team you are thinking of has very good individual players who have learned and practice the basics of their positions consistently on a day in and day out basis. Several of these same players may also perform their roles at exceptional levels on a regular basis. However, it is also likely that your favorite sports team would not be nearly as successful if it did not also work well together as a unit. When we consider successful sports teams or business teams, we see they do the following well as a unit:

1. They share roles and responsibilities.
2. They cooperate at high levels and compete with one another at low levels.
3. They analyze and evaluate their performance and provide feedback to each other.
4. They demonstrate openness and trust.
5. They encourage spontaneity and creativity.
6. They recognize individual and team accomplishments.
7. They anticipate problems.
8. They problem solve together.
9. They achieve results.
10. They advocate for themselves (as a team).

Title companies have a tendency to have both isolation within a team and fighting between the teams. In production teams, employees often work on individual files at various stages of the workflow and it is common for employees to become so focused on the intricacies of a file they become isolated from the other members of their team. Several years ago, a common joke was title examiners seldom came out to see the light of day when they were working on difficult files.

Across teams, we see any number of common complaints. For example, title and escrow teams often complain order entry gathers incomplete information and misspells seller names and addresses. Title teams complain the escrow staff do not proactively investigate curative matters thoroughly before calling title for help. Escrow teams complain title personnel are too slow, and everyone complains about sales staff making promises to customers before first checking with title and escrow. Of course, these are just a few examples, and there are many more. The critical idea is individuals do not view themselves as working as a part of a larger team, which is the company as a whole.

Guiding Principle

> **Title and escrow units often view themselves as independent and not working for the larger company team.**

In deciding if your work teams need development, we recommend that you start by considering the ability of the individual on the team and the **ability** of the team as a whole. Do the individual team members have all the skills required to do the work of the company successfully? If they do not, training may be necessary to improve basic technical skills.

Beyond ability, we consider the **intra-teamwork.** Have team members learned how to interact and perform successfully as a group? If they haven't, there is a wide range of team skills that managers need to develop, including team decision making, how to participate effectively in meetings, how to problem solve, how to evaluate team performance, how to communicate effectively, and how to ensure balanced participation on the team.

Often in title insurance companies, there is a very good intra teamwork, but poor **inter-teamwork.** Think about your title and escrow teams. Do they interface successfully with others? If they do not, it may be beneficial to require that team members visit and "job shadow" workers in other departments to "spend a day in someone else's shoes." Another idea is for teams to invite members from other teams to participate in their team meetings.

In many title insurance companies, some of the work teams, for example Title and Admin can feel isolated from the customers. Often the only people who see customers are sales people and closers. In evaluating each team, consider how effectively each team works with customers? If **external-teamwork** is an issue, your teams likely need training in what constitutes basic customer service and how to provide exceptional service.

Several years ago, we were in a team meeting where the leader complained that the group was not meeting expectations. However, the team knew there was one member of the team who was consistently making bad decisions, missing assignments and in general under-performing. The team also knew the leader did not like confrontation and had a very indirect leadership style. For several months, the team leader continued to reprimand the entire group while the frustration level on the team continued to rise. Over the years, we have seen this same scenario replicated by many managers who fail to correctly either diagnose an individual's team performance or choose not to confront a problem directly with an employee.

Determining whether poor team performance is actually based on one or two team members or the whole team is an important factor. If the performance of the team is being lowered by one or two individuals, the approach should be to work directly with those individuals and not the entire team. Managers who hesitate or fail to address individual team member performance directly will waste time and effort in declaring the issue a "team problem" and the team will more than likely resent the assertion.

Individual team members who under-perform may be doing so for a variety of reasons. Often the keys to improving a person's performance is a careful analysis of what the person is doing and not doing and the consequences and incentives that are either present or not present in the situation. Handling individual performance issues directly with the individual (and not the team) will be the correct solution.

You may also have team members who come from highly competitive backgrounds and who are more accustomed to working by themselves. They find, as team members, the very actions that got them ahead in the past are now contrary to the goals of the team. These individuals may have unique skills that will be beneficial, but their actions need to be directed by the manager so they are not counterproductive to team goals.

Guiding Principle

> **If team performance is being lowered by one or two individuals, work directly with those individuals and not the entire team.**

In the early 1990's we marveled at Phil Jackson's ability as a coach to build a championship basketball team with a group of players that had very different skill sets as well as personalities. Perhaps no person presented a greater challenge on the team than Dennis Rodman who was a highly competitive player but who also had his own ideas about almost everything. Jackson knew that Rodman had a special skill set that was critical to championship teams, he was a terrific rebounder. However, Jackson also knew there were certain behaviors he would need to manage with Rodman for him to be a good team player, while he could ignore others. For example, Jackson allowed Rodman to continue to dye his hair different colors, but he insisted that he come to practice on time, focus on team success and support his fellow team members.

One of the goals of every team manager is to produce optimal performance from each member. Optimal performance by individuals in a team setting means identifying and utilizing individual strengths. Jackson understood that Rodman was very much his own person with a distinctive personal style and he challenged him to use that style to be the best rebounder in the NBA. The challenge in managing the independent person lies in keeping what is best while establishing goals that require cooperative and supportive actions toward members of the team to achieve those goals. When the non-performing, independent or uncooperative individual impedes the achievement of team goals, their behavior must be dealt with directly. Finally, below are a few additional team development ideas to consider.

Self-Assessment. Have the team assess team behavior. Use the results from the assessment to identify team goals. We recommend that managers regularly observe their teams and team members and ask how they think the team is performing. The feedback can be instructive to both the manager and the team. The manager can use the feedback to adjust his direction, guidance and coaching and the team benefits from knowing what each other are thinking. For example, ask the team, during a meeting, to discuss their strengths and weaknesses as a group.

Guiding Principle

Ask the team to complete a self-assessment.

The manager can also adopt a more formal approach and ask the team to complete a team building survey. Team members can complete the survey anonymously on their own and then send the survey to the manager who can calculate the average group scores for each survey question. The manager can then report on the group results and lead a team discussion on what the team is doing well and where the team thinks it needs to make improvements.

For example, the following 15 statements can be used to assess teamwork. Read each statement and rate your agreement using a five-point rating scale in which a one means strongly disagree and five means strongly agree. If the group average rating on any question is below four, you have a potential area of team development.

1. The leader's management style matches the needs of the team.
2. Goals and objectives are clear to the team.
3. Communication is open and frequent.
4. Members offer frank, constructive criticism.
5. Roles within the team are clear.
6. There is a high degree of cooperation.
7. Creativity and motivation are evident.
8. Productivity and efficiency are high
9. Quality is consistently high.
10. Team members trust each other.
11. The team morale is positive.
12. Team members put forth their best efforts.
13. The team has fun together.
14. Customers like working with the whole team.
15. The team advocates for itself.

Team development day. This is an idea we have used with many teams throughout the years. We often suggest planning the day for when the weather will be good outside so that you can evoke a "picnic" or "retreat" type atmosphere by scheduling the use of a nearby park or resort where the team will feel like they are getting away from the office. During the day, we schedule several team building activities, a lunch for the team, and then end with a social gathering late in the afternoon or early evening. The day can be planned as both a time to discuss and work on team strengths and weaknesses and used as a reward for team performance well earned. There are several books available from your preferred business book source that list and provide instructions for team building exercises to use. We prefer activities that do not rely on a large degree of physical skill and focus more on creative team thinking and planning.

Team building activities. In addition to planning an outdoor team-building day, we also recommend conducting team-building activities during regularly scheduled team meetings. A team building activity will liven up a meeting agenda and often energize a group. You can choose an activity that will take not more than 15 or 20 minutes. If you include team-building activities in your meeting agenda on a regular basis, you will increase the probability that the team will look forward to meetings.

Managing Teams

When Roger was on the Faculty of Southern Illinois University (1986-1992), he managed a human service agency funded by the state of Illinois. John Lutzker created project 12-Ways in 1979 as a program providing more than 12 services to families with a history of child abuse and neglect. The main feature of the program was the parent trainers and therapists were graduate students in the Behavior Analysis Program at SIU. John was a dynamic leader who personally shaped the project for 10 years.

When John Lutzker left the program, Brandon Greene took the reins, and once again, the face and culture of the agency changed, taking on Brandon's personality and interests. Under Brandon's direction, the program became a significant part of the state of Illinois's Department of Children and Family Services budget. When Roger became the Operations Manager in 1987, the agency had a budget of over a million dollars and a staff of twenty.

In reflecting on his first management team experience, Roger recalls the first time he met with the 12-Ways staff. In the meeting, he jumped right in and talked about his role and the changes he and Brandon expected to bring about. The groups' response was characterized by one staff member who said, "We have heard this all before, and nothing is going to change. I was here before you arrived and I will be here after you are gone." Looking back on this experience it is clear that Roger had not read our next chapter on Starting to Manage. To begin with, Roger had spent little time learning about the company or staff. Therefore, in his first all staff meeting, the group did not know or trust Roger and had no reason to believe him, and every reason to fear him. It retrospect, it took over a year for the staff to trust Roger and for Roger to effectively manage and change the operation. Roger did manage to change Project 12-Ways during the five years he was COO and he was there after the employee who spoke up was long gone, but the culture of the agency 20 years later remains a reflection of its Director, Brandon Greene.

TAKE AWAY ACTIVITY
CHAPTER 6
DEVELOPING YOUR TEAM

1. We have discussed several development ideas for your work teams. Which ideas fit your needs or situation the best? List three ideas you can implement in some fashion with one or more of your work teams in the next three months.

2. Using our list of seven areas for management team development, evaluate the management team structure and processes that exist in your title insurance company and identify actions you need to take to address each area.

   a. Organizational chart

   b. Expectations

   c. Job descriptions and responsibilities

   d. Goals

   e. Team meetings

   f. Communication procedures

   g. Evaluative feedback

GUIDING PRINCIPLES
CHAPTER 6
DEVELOPING YOUR TEAM

1. In the title insurance industry, teamwork can lead to consistent approaches to customers, increased responsibility, ownership for products and services, and improvements in morale. In the end, the value of teamwork in a title insurance company is that it results in greater productivity and better service.

2. Set clear expectations for your management team members. Discuss with them what is expected in team meetings as well as on a daily basis.

3. Managers should have written job descriptions, responsibilities, and yearly goals that include a strong emphasis on team development and participation.

4. The power of a team is shown by what the group can accomplish as a whole and the assistance they can lend each other.

5. Provide frequent communications and evaluative feedback for manager behavior and performance.

6. In title and escrow teams, team members often view themselves as independent or not working for the larger team, which is the company as a whole.

7. If the performance of a team is being lowered by one or two individuals, the approach should be to work directly with those individuals and not the entire team.

8. Evaluate the strength of your team by asking the team to complete a self-assessment. Use the results to help determine development needs and set goals.

CHAPTER 7

EMPLOYEE CULTURE

The culture of a company is determined by the vision and values being promoted and lived, the leadership of the company, the employees and managers who make up the company, and the way work is performed. In order to develop a picture of the culture of some companies, you may even have to examine the customers who use that company and buy its products and services.

Employee culture means the mix of people at work, the number of women and men, the mix of race and ethnic identification along with and other demographics, for example the mix of young and old, experienced and inexperienced. All of these dimensions make up the employee culture. When authors talk about work culture, they mean "the way work is done around here."

Guiding Principle

Work culture means "the way work is done around here."

In Chapter 7, we focus on several factors that affect work and employee culture. We start the chapter by discussing hiring practices that ultimately shape your future workforce. Next, we tackle a topic that is often discussed with few specific answers, employee morale. We end the chapter by reviewing the difficult topic of downsizing and reducing hours and pay at times when these actions are necessary.

Most small title insurance companies today are likely to have more women than men, and most will have employees who have been with the company a long time or their entire career. On the east coast, in companies that focus only on the title abstract, commitment, or prelim, the culture will be dominated by the title and policy department. In the South, Southwest, and West, the culture of the company made be shaded more towards the escrow or settlement side of the business.

In the Midwest, both groups may fight for dominance, and in every company, there is likely to be a clash between the production departments (title and escrow) and sales.

Perhaps the single most important factor in shaping the culture of a small company is the person in charge, the owner, the founder, the boss. He or she will hire and possibly train all of the first generation employees. The people who will one day manage. In companies with a single owner, the culture of the company will very much resemble that person, his/her values and interests. For example, one very successful title insurance company in the west, the owner is famous for her charity work. Now so is her company. In another example, title insurance companies owned by lawyers often take on the language and demeanor of a law office, calling customers clients and talking about cases rather than files or orders.

Another feature that is coming to dominate title insurance companies and is shaping their culture is technology. Having up to date equipment, having web-based systems, having employees who understand and enjoy technology creates a company that seems to be moving forward. Companies that are still mastering email or texting and are not on Facebook, LinkedIn, or Twitter all face the risk of losing to a newer competitor.

Guiding Principle

> **Technology is shaping the work culture of the future.**

For us as Psychologists, the most interesting aspect of a company is its culture. Who is leading, who are the managers, how is the work managed, what are the problems, where are the conflicts, how is the work done around here. One way that we understand the culture of a company is to have every employee complete a DiSC personal profile. As previously discussed, the DiSC categorizes people as Dominate, Influencer, Steady, and Conscientious. By completing profiles on all the employees, we can create a picture of each department or team, and of the company as a whole. For example, if the owner is a Dominate person who likes to make it up as she goes and the majority of key employees are steady, we know the place will be productive and work together effectively. On the other hand, if the majority of employees are high C, conscientious, then we know there are likely to be real conflicts between the owner and the employees.

This scenario can be even worse when owners and employees are related.

Hiring for the future

In every culture, there is some type of expression that says, "Too many cooks can spoil a pot," meaning that too many chefs or too many leaders, managers, or people with dominate opinions will cause a problem at work. Likewise, a common expression says, "One bad apple can spoil a barrel." Meaning that it only takes one person to destroy a team. When hiring employees it is critical that the owner or manager doing the selection and hiring takes into account the nature of the work, the composition of the team if one exists, the culture of the company, and the future direction of the company.

Often times a new employee is hired because the company has a hole; it has work that is not being done. In this situation, it is natural to hire the first person who comes along because he or she has the technical knowledge. An employee with a lot of experience brings a lot of baggage with him/her. Sometimes experience in another company is invaluable, but only if the new hire is a good fit. Estimates are that a wrong hire will cost a company 1.5 to 3 times their salary for each year the person is at work. In our experience, the best hires occur when the recruitment and hiring process is broken down into a simple set of steps or rules.

1. Know who you are as a company.
2. Understand the job and work required.
3. Be clear on qualities for the job and company.
4. Be clear on job specific skills.
5. Advertise widely.
6. Require a completed job packet before screening.
7. Screen applicants – use a phone interview as a screen.
8. Interview top candidates using a written interview guide.
9. Score the interviewees.
10. Interview high scores a second time.
11. Never hire a candidate because you need a person.
12. Hire with a 3-month probationary period.

Interview Guide

In all our hiring interviews, we use some version of Brad Smart's, Smart Interview Guide. The most detailed guide includes a job application form, history, background check, and drug screening form, along with excellent interview questions taken from Smart's book, *Topgrading.* [4]

The interview guide in Topgrading is designed for executive hires, and may be too advanced for the average candidate in a title insurance company. We have used this form extensively and like it, however, we have designed additional questions specific to the title insurance industry.

In developing your company's set of interview questions, we recommend starting with the key questions in Topgrading and then look at Smart's earlier book on interviewing, *The Smart Interviewer* [5] and use part of the interview guide from that book.

In a down real estate market, where 10-20% of title professionals have been laid off and are looking for jobs, it is likely if you advertise, you will receive too many job applications. This fact, speaks to the need to create a set of standard forms, for example, a job application form with education and work history, a reference form, and other standard Human Resource forms. In addition, it is important to require a written (typed) resume. The information contained in these forms and the ways in which they are completed often provide a first level of screening. For example, does the person's resume contain spelling or grammar errors? Are there gaps in a person's work history? How recent are the references?

When faced with dozens or hundreds of applications we recommend that the first level of screening is completed by an HR administrator, or administrative assistant. Most large companies today complete their initial screenings on line and many work with recruitment agencies. This level of sophistication is beyond smaller title insurance companies, but you should have a jobs section on your website that provides interactive functions for perspective candidates. In addition, we suggest using phone interviews. A phone interview can last less than ten minutes and yet determine quite a bit about a person's history and experience. Finally, when the number of candidates is down

[4] Brad Smart. Topgrading: How Leading Companies Win by Hiring, Coaching, and Keeping the Best People, Revised and Updated Edition. New York, Portfolio Hardcover, 2005.
[5] Brad Smart. The Smart Interviewer [Paperback]. New York, Wiley, 1990

to three to five, we recommend interviews with the manager, owners, and sometimes with a team.

One of the things we encounter most often is the owner who wants to conduct an interview with a blank piece of paper (no prepared questions) and who likes to make quick decisions. An owner who will hire without talking to everyone on the final list. These owners often hire a real gem, but they also have employees they would like to fire who have worked for the company five, ten, or twenty years.

In our experience starting out with the same set of questions places every candidate on an equal footing. Bringing a candidate back for a second interview means you can now ask the tough questions. Also, bringing a candidate back for a second interview means you can ask the person to perform some aspect of their future work, for example, answer a phone call or examine a file. Creating an on-the-job skills test is one of the best ideas we know, yet it is not used, because someone has to create the test, and making the candidate take a test can be uncomfortable.

Guiding Principle

> **Create an on the job skills test to gauge how a prospect will perform in the future.**

The other thing that greatly aids in hiring is contacting references and past managers. Calling a previous employer to check on a potential hire takes less than fifteen minutes and the worst thing that can happen is the employer says it is against their policy to discuss past employees.

Assessing Employees and Performance

When we think of culture, we think about the mix of people, the mix of personal styles, the performance of the company, and the performance of each individual. In effectively managed companies, there will be established procedures for evaluating employees on an annual basis. When we evaluate the culture of a company, we talk to each employee, and if they exist, we examine the performance review system. Unfortunately, in many small companies annual reviews for every employee can be missing. Interestingly, the group who most often lacks annual performance reviews are managers.

If your company or a group of employees are in need of an annual performance review, this is one of the first things we try to install, because it is a critical aspect of employee morale. If your company lacks a review process, we strongly recommend seeking HR advice and we want to emphasize that a performance review need have nothing to do with salary decisions. With all our clients, we emphasized that employees' need feedback regarding their performance. Feedback at least on an annual basis. Salary decisions on the other hand are business decisions and should be performed on a regular basis and they should take advantage of a recent review, but never be tied to the review. If you have an older process in place, that is not fully used, we recommend adopting one of the new online systems, because of their ease of use and the quality of the on-line process.

Employee Morale

For managers, the concept of morale can be elusive. Does having good morale mean having happy employees? Can you have high morale and high productivity? Although good morale can be easy to recognize when you experience it, it can be difficult to define or measure. Likewise, even when it is easy to see that morale is low, the task of improving morale can seem daunting, where to start, what to change? Despite the difficulty in defining, measuring, and changing morale, we know that creating and maintaining good morale is one key ingredient to a company's success, especially during difficult times.

Guiding Principle

> *Maintaining good morale is a key to a company's success.*

Consider for a minute two title insurance companies, Bad Title Company (BTC) and Good Title Company (GTC). The two companies started in 1990 and both are located on the main street in a small Midwestern city. Like other title insurance companies, in the last 15 months, each company experienced a significant decrease in orders and revenue, and each went through a difficult layoff, losing more than 15% of their workforce.

As the market recovers, the owner of each company asked, "Is my company ready for a recovery?" At BTC, the office physical environment appears run down. The carpets look worn and the walls need painting. Beyond appearances, the company is having employee problems. For example, a number of the most experienced employees seem to be constantly complaining about the company, customers, and the less experienced employees. Among their complaints is the fact that there have been no raises in three years, they complain that the owner is gone a lot, and they say they are overworked. As an example of the bad feelings among staff, the title staff created a separate lunch area, just for title staff. In addition to employee complaints, the company has a higher than normal level of absenteeism and employees being late to work. In terms of production, the title Department has high turn times and the escrow files have errors that have to be corrected at the last minute.

At GTC things are a little different. Employees are less experienced, but they are well trained; they show up early, stay late, and often mention, "Loving their job." Everyone eats in the same area and once a week there is a potluck, and once a quarter a team dinner or breakfast. The company recently renovated its office, making the environment warmer and more comfortable for customers. Each day there is a daily staffing, and everyone, including the owner and managers, work in one large area. Among the employees, there are the typical gripes and complaints, and not everyone likes everyone else, but most employees' say they feel appreciated and respected, and many comment they have at least one friend at work.

If you were to bet on which company will recover first, which would you choose? If you were a customer looking for a new place to close or an unemployed title professional looking for a job, which company would you choose? Of course, the answer is GTC. If you were to guess which company had better employee morale, it would be easy to guess. Why? The answer is simple; leadership and management practices have been designed, to create a positive work environment and positive employee behavior.

In our experience, employee morale is affected by a number of factors. While, no single factor or solution may be sufficient to improve morale, experience tells us a single factor can significantly lower morale. For example, in colleges and universities, the chairperson of a department or the dean of a college is typically elected and often is hired from the outside. Hiring the wrong leader can throw a cohesive, competent, productive faculty in chaos. Likewise, promoting the wrong person to manage a title department or hiring the wrong closer can tear apart an existing team. This observation suggests that who you hire to manage and who you hire to do the work are obviously critical factors affecting employee morale. Other factors are listed below.

Factors Affecting Morale:
- Employees hired
- Type of work
- Training
- Work methods
- Managers
- Management practices
- Work environment
- Customer behavior
- Leadership

In companies with very high morale, the owners, managers, and employees are typically doing all kinds of things right and it may be hard to improve on what exists, whereas in companies with very low morale, the owners, managers, and employees may be doing so many things wrong that they might be better off starting over from scratch.

Perhaps the company that faces the greatest challenge is the "Average" company. These companies get the work out and make money, but there is no vitality or spark among the employees and many feel like they are just filling in a space. In these companies, customers would rate the service they receive as "Good," not great. The difficulty for an Average company is they cannot afford to start from scratch; rather they have to start with what they have and build from there.

If your company feels like it is "just getting by," then it may be time to formally assess employee morale and evaluate how your leadership and management practices are contributing to morale.

The best way to assess employee morale is to focus on behavior at work. Several business authors have suggested that many of the behaviors associated with high employee morale are linked to the concept of employee engagement. They argue that in companies where employees are engaged, morale is high.

The Ritz-Carlton Hotel Company[6], for example, believes the more engaged their employees are the greater likelihood they will be more creative and able to perform at higher standards. Using a survey process, the Ritz-Carlton measures employee engagement on a regular basis. In their surveys, the hotels with the highest levels of staff engagement were among their best producing hotels, in terms of revenue and bottom-line results. At the Ritz Carlton hotels, having engaged employees is not an accident. Their recruitment and training process is intensive and they have a high level of empowerment and accountability combined with frequent assessment and measurement.

Assessing Morale

Creating a formal process for assessing employee morale like the Ritz Carlton does, may be more than you need at this moment, so here is a simpler process. Consider the twenty questions presented in Table 5 on the next page.

To get started, try observing these behaviors as you walk through the office. Observe when you hold staff meetings. During these times, listen to employees as they talk with and about customers. When you have the opportunity, sit in on closings, and then talk to customers. Finally, talk with your employees individually and ask them about how they feel about the company.

When you are done, if you can answer "Yes" to the majority of the twenty questions it is likely your employees are engaged and employee morale is high. If, on the other hand, you answered "No" to more than half the questions, it is likely you have a morale problem, and need to consider how your leadership, management, and business practices are affecting morale.

We said in our introduction that employee morale is affected by several factors and no single factor is likely to affect every employee. Nonetheless, we know that employee engagement is a key to success. Table 5. Employee Morale Questions.

1. Is work finished early or on time?
2. Is work accurate and complete?

---

6 Michelli, Joseph A., *The New Gold Standard: 5 Leadership Principles for Creating a Legendary Customer Experience Courtesy of The Ritz-Carlton Hotel Company*. New York: McGraw-Hill, 2008, (pp.127).

3. Is work consistent?
4. Do employees say positive things about the company?
5. Do employees say they enjoy their work?
6. Do employees talk positively about customers?
7. Do employees have friends at work?
8. Do employees interact with each other often?
9. Do employees initiate actions without being asked or told?
10. Do employees volunteer to help others in various ways?
11. Do employees offer new ideas or solutions to problems?
12. Do employees get excited when the company, a team, or individual staff member has a success?
13. Are employees enthusiastic, pleasant, or cheerful?
14. When asked would employees say, "I have what I need to get my job done successfully."
15. Would they recommend your company to their friends?
16. Do they believe their supervisor or manager cares about them?
17. Do they believe in the company's future?
18. Do they participate at meetings?
19. Are employee complaints about work or the work environment few in frequency?
20. Do employees get excited when they receive a compliment?

Here is a list of ideas for managers to consider that have been shown to engage staff and improve morale.

Set clear expectations. People often want structure in their work lives and many employees are goal driven, meaning they are affected by goals and will strive to achieve goals.

Set team goals. As a part of your employee review process, develop professional development goals with individual employees. Assign special projects or initiatives to targeted staff and set project goals with timelines. For each production team set monthly and quarterly goals.

Hold team meetings. Conduct daily, weekly, and monthly team meetings and make sure the employees view the meetings as effective and useful. Managers often say that employees hate meetings or they have no time for meetings. The truth is everyone hates a purposeless meeting, that is, a meeting that wastes your time, but few people dislike a meeting where their ideas and opinions are solicited.

Efficient meetings, meetings with a purpose, meeting where ideas are shared, where decisions are made, are usually judged worthwhile

Put employee welfare at the top of your list. Let employees take care of customers, the manager's job is to take care of employees. The job of the manager is to make sure that employees have all the tools necessary to do their best work. Employee morale will be low in companies where managers and team leaders spend more time focused on personally serving customers or earning personal incentives, than they spend on teaching staff and standardizing work processes.

Be caring, honest, direct, and sincere. No one can be happy or productive working for a dictator. Likewise, no one can be happy working for someone who is a pushover. Employees want a solid manager who is honest and will stand up for their interests. Perhaps worst of all is working for or with someone who is disingenuous, blames others, or lies.

Be a role model. Become more engaged in training and providing a model for how employees should work with customers. The key is to act, as you want your employees to act. Talk positively about customers and the work. Never talk negatively about other employees or about customers. Look for opportunities to model the behavior you want. For example, meet customers at the door in the reception area. Stay late with a closer to help with a closing. Go on a sales call with another staff member. Roll up your sleeves and examine a difficult file during a high volume period. Pick up a commitment and hand-deliver it to a targeted customer or send a special note with an electronic transmittal of a document.

Be accessible. Communicate and interact with your employees daily. Walk the floor and talk with each employee several times a day (where possible). Grab your coffee first thing in the morning and circulate among cubicles or offices. Try to pick a standard time during the day when your door is always open. If you do this consistently and make a point of it, the message will get through to your staff.

Ask questions and be a good listener. Solicit and act on employee ideas. Staff will be more motivated if they see their input is valued and acted on. It is always better for a manager to use an employee idea because it builds ownership and pride. We always recommend managers to ask for employee ideas first.

Ask for feedback from staff. We encourage managers to ask for constructive / positive feedback about their performance and behavior. At the end of a staff meeting, ask, "How do you think our team is doing?" "What can I do to be a better resource for you?"

Provide frequent encouragement and praise. Remember that rewards do not have to be money and the best rewards happen right after the behavior occurs. There is a simple concept called "catch 'em being good." It means praise the behavior you want when you see it. Do not wait until later. If you observe an employee demonstrating great service behavior, praise their behavior immediately.

Show how work contributes to the larger company. For example, the purpose of the receptionist is not to check someone in for a closing; it is to create an exceptional first experience. Create opportunities for employees to perform at their best. Most employees are good at several jobs or tasks, and great at one thing. Arrange it so that every employee has the chance to be great once a day.

Focus on the natural leaders. Identify the natural leaders in your teams to help build and maintain enthusiasm. We recommend selecting different staff members to lead staff meetings and co-chair special projects or events.

Get employees involved in your community. Successful companies, Starbucks, for example, have found that employee morale is high when community involvement is an important part of the business model. Community activities sponsored by your business are a feel good activity that makes your employees proud of who they work for and where they work. It helps build company loyalty and gets your employees talking and thinking about your company in positive ways. Community involvement also fosters creativity and initiative among employees and is great for team building. Here are a few examples we have seen recently. Organize a company team for a charity walk or run and print up team-company shirts. Participate in a charity silent auction and donate some fun activity that staff can participate in like 20 free car washes performed by employees. Organize a "Toys for Tots" campaign for needy families, around a seasonal holiday. Participate in United Way or Habitat for Humanity.

Treat employees as professionals and adults. Employees want a work environment that is structured (rules and procedures) but they also want, and need, to be given control over their work and choices in their work. They need to be treated with respect and expected to act like adults and professionals in return.

Creating Culture

In the last chapter, we mentioned Roger's first management experience at Project 12-Ways. In 1989, in addition to his position on the Faculty at SIU and serving as COO of Project 12-ways, Roger started Parents That Care (PTC). Parents That Care was a group parent-training program for families with a history of child abuse or neglect. Unlike Project 12-Ways, the PTC staff were hand selected from people who Roger had worked with and who liked and trusted Roger as much as he liked and trusted them. In PTC, the staff worked with Roger to design the program and its services. Parents in the program attended a meeting where a meal and childcare were provided while the parents learned about good parenting skills. The agency and its culture were as much a reflection of the staff as Roger. Roger and the staff cooked the meals, provided training and childcare, and transported families. In Parents That Care, Roger was able to start from scratch. He hired the staff and together they created the procedures and practices for the agency. In PTC, Roger could be compared to the owner of a small title insurance agency in that he was CEO, manager, team member, and chief bottle washer. Parents That Care ended in 1992 when a summer battle over state funding temporarily shut down many programs. Reading the writing on the wall, Roger helped his staff find other jobs and he left the University for a job consulting with COBA.

In all the time Roger managed, he had the pleasure of hiring dozens of new staff and building a work culture. Along the way, he also faced the task of firing a few employees, but he never had to go through a large-scale downsizing. Downsizing is an action that always affects employee culture and morale and as such needs to be carefully planned and executed.

Downsizing

In general, if you are planning to reduce staff, employment consultants recommend that you make, one deep cut rather than making a series of small cuts. A series of small cuts can have a very negative effect on staff morale. It will be better to make staff cuts in a systematic way that does not belabor an already difficult process by slowly stretching the cuts out over a long agonizing period.

Our recommendation is to know what your labor ratios need to be to meet both your financial goals, and your customer service requirements. Then, make the necessary staff cuts in a timely way that does not prolong the psychological stress the reductions will have on the staff that remain.

In most title insurance companies, the first step to reducing labor expense is to eliminate non-essential, unproductive, and problem employees. This action should be taken regardless of the economy or the success of the company and we continually urge owners and managers to evaluate employee performance so that they can identify non-performers and take appropriate action. Of course, in hard times, owners and managers have a tendency to ignore or work around employees that are not performing up to standard, particularly if the employee has a long history with the company. In our opinion, good times or bad, non-performing employees have to be released for the good of the larger team.

It is our experience, most productive employees welcome this type of action because they feel the unproductive or problem employee(s) are hampering the rest of the team and setting a bad example. Overall employee morale can suffer when employees see there is a team member who is not doing his\her fair share.

We have worked with a number of title insurance agencies helping them develop and implement a performance review system whose purpose, in part, was to establish performance ratings for the different positions in a company. These systems typically require the agency to set minimum performance standards for employees.

In good times, when an established employee is inconsistent in his/her performance or is performing below a standard, the company should follow a prescribed set of Human Resource steps (those specified in the company's policy manual). For example:
1. Provide performance feedback and set a prescribed timeline for improvement. Include a written warning.
2. Provide remedial assistance or training. Include a written warning.
3. Give a final written warning and set a prescribed timeline for improvement.
4. Terminate, if no improvement is made.

Likewise, when an established employee is consistently performing below an established performance standard the company should take more immediate action provided it has provided performance feedback and set a prescribed timeline for improvement. In bad times, these employees should be terminated.

When considering any staff reductions, you should first determine which positions are essential, and which employees are essential in those positions. Your goal in evaluating people is to identify a core group of strong employees who you believe will be most instrumental in helping you weather the storm and achieve success for the future.

We have already stated that if you are going to reduce your labor force you should follow the one deep cut philosophy, but we need to add a second word of caution. Sometimes in making staff cuts, an owner or manager will follow the last in, first out strategy, eliminating the most recent hires and entry-level staff, people with the least training or experience. Typically, these new and entry-level employees represent the smallest percentage of a company's total salary expense. As hard as it is, an owner has to evaluate every job critically and every employee, carefully looking at the person's performance and at the impact of eliminating their salary. This means eliminating any high salaried employee who does not meet your performance standards.

In eliminating the newest, least experienced, or lowest paid employees, a company also runs the risk of letting a new talented employee go who may be much better suited or skilled to meet the company's future.

Guiding Principle

> ### *A last in, first out strategy is not always wise.*

A systematic way to evaluate which employees are critical for your future is to rate them across several skills or competency dimensions that pertain to the future success of your business. This process should be systematic and fairly assess every employee, but it does not need to be difficult or cumbersome. We recommend evaluating all title and escrow employees using a core set of 9-12 dimensions. Managers, sales staff, and administrative staff may need to be evaluated on additional or different dimensions.

Listed below are the dimensions we recommend for evaluating title and escrow employees, managers, and sales employees,

EMPLOYEE DIMENSIONS

1. Adaptability/flexibility/ Initiative
2. Communication
3. Computer / technology skills
4. Customer service
5. Dependability
6. Integrity\ethics
7. Job knowledge
8. Productivity
9. Quality of work
10. Teamwork / people skills

MANAGER DIMENSIONS
1. Achieves results
2. Business and financial knowledge and ability
3. Decision making / judgment
4. Leadership
5. Operational management
6. People management
7. Sales and marketing ability
8. Sense of urgency
9. Strategic thinking

SALES DIMENSIONS
1. Achieving sales goals
2. Customer focus
3. Interpersonal skills
4. Listening skills
5. Negotiation skills
6. Problem solving\analysis
7. Product knowledge
8. Sales planning
9. Teamwork
10. Territory management

Each of these dimensions can be evaluated using a five point rating scale and the results can then be compared within positions and across employees. Omitted from the example are length of employment and salary. In our opinion, each employee should first be evaluated on their job performance using these dimensions and then salary and length of employment comes into play when evaluating the poorest scoring employees in each position.

Supervisors and managers could be evaluated using the first ten employee dimensions, however there are nine additional dimensions we use that are specific to managing. In our opinion, each manager should first be evaluated on their job performance using a combination of the nineteen dimensions and only then should salary and length of employment comes into play when evaluating the poorest scoring employees in any each position.

Evaluating your workforce on a simple set of performance dimensions can become one component in your annual evaluations of employees. In good times or bad, it is important to balance having the right staff in place for the present with having the right people for the future. If you are considering a staff reduction, it is essential to consider managers and supervisors in addition to line staff. The list provides an example of dimensions for evaluating sales staff.

If a title or escrow manager is a mediocre manager, but a great performer, you may be better off eliminating their management responsibilities and salary, but keeping him or her on the work team. When a manager is personally unproductive or his/her team is unproductive, you face a different issue. If the person is a good people manager, he or she may simply need stronger performance goals or more accountability. When a manager shows poor people management and has poor performance, it is time to let the person go.

If your company has one office with a small staff, for example, with one person in each core position, it may be impossible to do anything but reduce hours or salary. As the market recovers, a good sales person will be positioned to take advantage quickly of the new opportunities that he/she has nurtured. Sales staffs who spend a disproportionate amount of time on maintaining existing customers and fail to develop new opportunities are not putting you in the best position for the future.

Companies with a small number of employees face a different situation from companies with a large work force. Likewise, companies with one location and a large work force divided into departments or functions may have to make different decisions when compared to companies with multiple offices and a duplication of functions in each office.

In companies with one location, a long-term approach to lowering staff expense may be cross training and combining staff responsibilities where possible. In companies with multiple full service offices and a duplication of staff positions in each office, centralization of production functions may be a viable alternative to consider. Functional areas like order entry, customer service, title and policy production and certain aspects of escrow processing are all suitable for centralization.

Guiding Principle

> ### *A redesign in workflow is critical to production centralization efforts.*

Besides a reduction in salary expense, centralizing a workforce needs to result in more efficient and productive work. As a part of any effort to centralize key functions within a title insurance company, it will be critical to examine and redesign the workflow being centralized. In many title insurance companies, the title production staff are already centralized whereas the escrow staffs are not. Simply moving your escrow processing staff in one location and then letting them perform work the way they always have is very likely a formula for disaster.

If done correctly, centralizing a work force allows you to eliminate redundant positions, whereas redesigning the workflow of a unit will result in greater efficiency and productivity gains by eliminating extra steps in the production process, reducing errors that cause re-work, and increasing or improving the use of technology.

Reducing Staff Hours or Pay

If you eliminate non-performing, redundant, and non-essential staff and your labor expense is still too high, your immediate approach will be reducing staff hours or staff pay. This is especially true if you have reached the tipping point where product quality or service levels would suffer from further elimination of individuals or positions.

If further staff reductions will lead to a significant decrease in your abilities to produce a quality product or adequately service your customers, then reducing paid hours spread systematically throughout the company should be considered. The key in reducing hours is to stagger who works fewer hours and when. To the extent possible, your customers need to continue to experience a fully functioning operation. If your company has one office with a small staff, for example, with one person in each core position, it may be impossible to do anything but reduce hours or salary. Throughout the period of time when reductions in staff, hours, or pay are occurring, communications regarding what is being done and why are critical.

Communications should be direct, honest and hopeful about the future. The management staff needs to be on the same page in terms of providing a sound rationale for the reductions and providing the necessary details. Some communications can include email notification, but any plan to reduce hours or salary should be communicated in a face-to-face meeting where employees have the opportunity for questions and answers. All communications need to include positive statements about how the agency is preparing for the future and a recovering market.

When the time comes to return hours, reverse salary changes, or add new staff, the same care needs to be taken in communicating to employees. Ultimately, your leadership out of a down market must continue to be driven by the staffing levels that are necessary to meet your labor ratio and financial goals and an undying eye toward providing support and direction for your most important resource, your employees.

TAKE AWAY ACTIVITY
CHAPTER 7
EMPLOYEE CULTURE

1. Answer the 20 questions presented in Table 5 as either yes or no. Record the number of Yes _____ and No _____. If you have more than 10 questions checked yes, your employees are engaged.

2. Use the list of 10 dimensions for employees to evaluate your escrow and title staff using the five point rating scale below.

3. Use the list of nine dimensions for managers to evaluate your management staff using the five point rating scale below.

4. Use the list of 10 dimensions for sales to evaluate your sales staff using the five point rating scale below.

Rating Scale

1 = never meets performance and behavior expectations

2 = occasionally meets performance and behavior expectations

3 = meets performance and behavior expectations

4 = occasionally exceeds performance and behavior expectations

5 = exceeds performance and behavior expectations

GUIDING PRINCIPLES
CHAPTER 7
EMPLOYEE CULTURE

1. Work culture means "the way work is done around here."

2. Technology is shaping the work culture of the future.

3. Create an on the job skills test to gauge how a prospect will perform in the future.

4. Creating and maintaining good morale is a key to a company's success.

5. Labor ratios, financial goals and customer service levels are useful in determining needed reductions in staffing.

6. A last in, first out strategy is not always wise.

7. A redesign in workflow is critical to production centralization efforts.

8. Assess your staff based on your future workforce skill and competency needs.

CHAPTER 8

STARTING TO MANAGE

Effective management in a title insurance company is a balance of technical knowledge and experience combined with the ability to affect people. Managing a new group or managing for the first time can be a daunting task. In the title insurance industry, more often than not, employees are moved into management and supervisory positions because they are experienced examiners or closers, but not because of their ability or potential to manage others. In our experience, acquiring technical knowledge and skills seldom prepare an employee to manage successfully.

Guiding Principle

> *Acquiring technical knowledge and skills seldom prepares an employee to manage successfully.*

Many small businesses often promote their best technical people to be supervisors and managers, and then provide no training, guidance, or support. Essentially, they place their best employees in a sink or swim situation. In smaller title insurance companies, the first person promoted to be a manager is often a son, daughter, or the most senior employee. In the rare case, a company will hire someone from the outside, someone with actual management experience or management potential. Whether promoted from within or hired from outside, there are a number of important actions a new manager can take to begin managing a team.

In Chapter 8, we consider the first three months of managing, whether it is a first position or simply a new group. Next we discuss the importance of understanding your management style. We end the chapter with a checklist of management tactics useful for new managers as well as seasoned managers.

The First 90 Days

The first day on the job as a manager is like the first day at a new school. There is a lot to do, a lot to learn, and it is easy to start out on the wrong foot. It is important for the new manager to have a plan for the first day, the first week, month and quarter. The plan may be driven significantly by the overall context of the new manager's appointment, the person's relationship to the team, and whether specific goals and objectives with timelines have been assigned. If the manager is turning around a failing business or saving a dysfunctional team, the pressure to get results will take precedent for the new manager, but in general, our advice is to take the time necessary to discover what makes the office or team tick. In general, title and escrow employees are people who like structure, rules, and process. They often are steady people who like doing things their way. Rushing in and immediately making a lot of changes is typically not the best way to build employee confidence and trust.

Any time a new manager has to enter a new work environment, he/she has to analyze the new situation. Having worked in a team is different from coming into a team as the new manager. Managing a successful team is different from managing a failing team.

Guiding Principle

It is important for the new manager to have a plan for the first day, the first week, month and quarter.

We recently helped a new Escrow Office Manager, for a prominent title insurance company in the Midwest, develop a 90-day transition plan for her new appointment. It is always a good idea for the new manager to tell the team that "we" are going to take 60-90 days to establish and implement a plan. That does not mean you do not expect action and results right away, it just means there will be a period of adjustment. In establishing a 90-day plan, you are sending a strong message to your employees that you are starting with no preconceived ideas about your office or team performance and that you will need their input, advice, and cooperation.

In the first weeks of the plan, it is critical to watch, listen, and ask. Interviewing and talking with your employees and getting out in the workspace to observe workflow makes you immediately visible and accessible to your employees. In large part, the message the new manager needs to send in the first 90 days is that you are there to listen and learn.

In the first months, the new manager is under the microscope. Employees are looking to see if the new manager will make the grade or fail. Employees respect a manager who is visible, a manager who takes an active role in understanding office issues. During the first 90 days, the more assurance you provide, the more respect and trust you will foster. Nonetheless, a team expects action, and will respect a new manager who gets quick and apparent results.

ON BEING A NEW MANAGER
Amy Everett is an Escrow Office Manager at
Meridian Title Company in Indiana.

Here are Amy's thoughts about being a first time manager.

"Becoming a new escrow manager proved to be a challenge for many reasons and I had a lot of questions. I knew I had to have a plan that included gaining input from each employee and observing their work.

My first fear was my predecessor had been there for 30 plus years! How would the employees feel about me stepping in to take over? Would they support me in my new role? How would I ever get them to have confidence in me?

There were 20 employees in the office and I knew I had to make sure they worked as a team. How would I get them to have respect for one another as co-workers? What could I do to motivate them to do the best job that they can?

The customers were a very big factor to consider as well and I had some of the same fears with them. Some Real Estate Agents and Lenders had been in the business and working with our company for many years. How would I gain their confidence and trust?"

Amy Everett's 90 Day Transition Plan

The following are the steps Amy Everett completed in her first 90 days as a new escrow manager:

1. Met with her immediate supervisor to plan the transition and identify the steps that would be followed.
   - ✓ Met with previous office manager to gain insights and opinions.
2. Asked company owner (CEO) and immediate supervisor to attend first employee office meeting.
   - ✓ Explained her transition goals for the first 90 days.
   - ✓ Discussed the steps of the transition plan.
   - ✓ Explained that employee input was critical to the success of the transition.
3. Interviewed each office employee individually.
   - ✓ The interviews lasted approximately 60 minutes and were confidential.
   - ✓ The purpose of the interview was for the new manager to listen to each employee and learn about roles and responsibilities.
   - ✓ The interviews included discussion on what the office did well and office issues from the employees' perspective.
   - ✓ The new manager used a standard list of questions in all the interviews to be consistent.
4. Sat with each employee at their work location to observe and ask questions about the employee's functions and to see the workflow first hand.
   - ✓ The observation sessions were scheduled separately from the interviews.
5. Developed a communication plan to announce the new appointment to customers.
   - ✓ The new manager worked with the sales group to plan the announcements and schedule joint customer visits with sales staff to introduce the new manager.
6. Scheduled time to research and observe specific functions in the office.
   - ✓ The reception area.
   - ✓ The phone system.
   - ✓ The computer platform for escrow processing.
   - ✓ Closings.
   - ✓ The workflow for communications to and from lenders for lender packages.
   - ✓ The procedures for curative work between escrow and title production.
7. Reviewed all reports and planning documents for the office.
   - ✓ Weekly and monthly performance reports.
   - ✓ Sales and Market Plans.
   - ✓ Customer target lists, including new customer targets.
   - ✓ Past employee performance appraisals.
   - ✓ Development goals for specific employees.
8. Analyzed results of all completed employee interviews and observations.
   - ✓ Made a list of strengths and weaknesses for office.
   - ✓ Prioritized list of office issues.
   - ✓ Discussed results with immediate supervisor.
   - ✓ Developed short and longer-term goals for office based on employee and supervisor input.
9. Met with the office team to share results of interviews and observations and discuss office goals.
   - ✓ Reviewed general results of interviews and observations.
   - ✓ Discussed office priorities and goals.
   - ✓ Discussed her management style and her expectations for the office.
   - ✓ Presented and acknowledged team accomplishments during her initial tenure.
   - ✓ Discussed what her daily and weekly schedule would be as a manager going forward.
10. Set timelines on when she would regularly get back with staff to review and discuss office progress and ask for additional employee feedback.

Consultants who are experts in organizational change know the demonstration of short-term gains or improvements is critical to the success of a new project. New managers need to consider the same concept. Throughout the first few weeks and months of a transition plan, the new manager should identify short-term improvements and accomplishments to celebrate with the team when they occur. In general, employees who are proficient in their work require very little management. What they seek in a manager is someone who will listen, who will fight for them, and who gets results.

Guiding Principle

The demonstration of short-term gains, improvements and success is critical for the new manager in the first 90 days.

Understanding Your Management Style

A big part of a new managers' first year is establishing a beachhead with employees in areas like trust, confidence, and open communications. Understanding your management style and how your style affects others is important.

Each of us has different styles of navigating through our environments and managers are no exception at work. Some managers are direct, to the point, results and action oriented, while other managers approach their work by focusing on teamwork, consensus building, and being patient. Still other managers are enthusiastic and sociable while others are calmer and introverted.

As behavioral psychologists, we believe that people's behaviors are shaped throughout their lifetimes by an interaction between their learning environments and the predispositions they have because of their genetic make-up. In effect, we believe a person's biology and their experiences create one or more styles or patterns of behaving. Think of these general patterns as behavior tendencies managers routinely exhibit in different situations.

The following four basic manager styles describe the behavior tendencies of many new managers, as well as, experienced managers. Which of these manager types describes managers whom you have known? Which of these manager types describes your behavior tendencies?

Direct Manager will want to charge in, and "start taking names and kicking butts." This manager may over manage or micro manage. The problem with a direct style is that it is unlikely to gain supporters. On the positive side, direct managers tend to be action and results oriented and to the point.

Indirect Manager will want to take the time to learn about the employees, gain their input about what is working well and what is not, learn about issues and obstacles. The problem with indirect managers often is that they take too long to make a decision.

Delegating Manager will always try to get results through others first. The delegating manager makes assignments and holds people accountable. This style works when employees are willing, capable, and ready to work.

Do-it-Yourself Manager will try to solve problems by personally bringing in orders or customers. Rather than show, delegate, or tell others what work to do, this manager will do the work. Of course, this manager is not really managing.

The person with no management experience still brings his/her basic behavioral style into the situation, but they have the potential to adopt any or all of the common management styles. We believe that it is important for managers to know and understand these behavior tendencies. In other words, it is important for managers to understand their management styles in specific work situations. If managers know and understand their behavior tendencies, they can be in a better position to adjust them when needed.

Guiding Principle

> *If managers know and understand their behavior tendencies, they can be in a better position to adjust them when needed.*

For example, if a manager has a tendency to be results oriented and direct, but she knows the employee needs to talk, then the manager can choose to adjust her style to fit the situation. Taking time to listen to the employee and get more details before offering her own opinion. Aligning your style to fit with the behavior tendencies of the employees you manage also requires that you have a way to consider employee behavior tendencies.

There are several commercially available systems designed to help managers evaluate their management styles as well as the behavior tendencies of the people they manage. We particularly like the DiSC Personal Profile system published by Inscape Publishing. The DiSC enables managers to assess their own behavioral tendencies as well as the employees they work with.

The New Manager Checklist

There are several additional tactics new managers should consider to gain and build trust. These concepts are important for all managers to consider, but they are especially important for the new manager. We have compiled a list of topics for you to use. As you go through our list, check off the tactics that fit your needs and situation.

Be Honest, Direct and Follow-Through. When employees ask for advice, for example, help in finding a solution for a problem file, many new managers will not know the immediate answers. Not always knowing the answers is to be expected and is only natural. The best advice for the new manager is to be direct and honest: "I do not know the answer to your question, but I will research it for you and get back to you within the hour." The new manager must understand they are not expected to be the expert and know all the answers. If the new manager is direct, honest and to the point, they will gain the respect of the employees who will be counting on them for help and direction. Consistency also is a key factor for the new manager. If you say you are going to do something, then you must follow-through to be an effective manager.

Be Accessible. New managers need to be visible and readily accessible to their employees. We often challenge new managers to indicate, on a daily and weekly basis, how and when they will be accessible and visible to their employees. We ask them to show us on their daily calendars using hourly time blocks.

The new manager also needs to communicate to employees when and how he will be accessible. We like to think back to our college days and the professors who posted their office hours on their doors. As students, we always knew the specific times of the day and week we could catch the professor to ask an important question. Employees are no different, they need to know how and when they can communicate with their manager. For example:

- I answer emails three times each day: first thing in the morning, noon, and at the end of the day.

- If my door is open, I am available. When it is closed I am not to be disturbed.

- I will hold a 15-minute 'huddle' in the middle of the office each morning.

- When I leave the office, my assistant will know how I can be reached.

- I will distribute my calendar at the beginning of each week.

Listen Well. Chris often tells the story of when he was a first time manager. He often thought he knew the answer before the employee finished the question. He was impatient, aggressive and always in a hurry. He never really listened well and often gave that impression to many of the employees who came to him for help. He knows now that he was making some of the classical mistakes new managers make when they think they are listening well but are not really. Here are a few basic listening techniques:

- <u>Do not talk first.</u> If you are talking you are not listening. Let the employee have their say. You will be surprised what you will hear if you do not interrupt.

- <u>Use silence to your advantage.</u> Often an employee will have more to say if you pause or allow a little silence before you speak. Pausing for a moment of silence often sends the signal to the employee that you truly want to hear everything they have to offer.

- Use direct eye contact. When you listen look at the person directly. You should not be busy on your computer, on your phone, or have your nose in some paper or report. Many teenagers these days have their thumbs going wildly on smart phones all most constantly when you try talking with them. Should the new mantra be, "Thumbs up, head up"?

- Acknowledge what you have heard. Use physical gestures, like nodding your head, or short verbal confirmations, to indicate you heard what the employee has to say. When the employee is finished, try repeating back to the employee the essence of what you have heard. Try saying, "This is what I heard you say... is that correct?" If the employee indicates you have not heard correctly, listen again.

- Be patient. Listening is time well spent by the manager. If you rush the employee you may not hear all that you need to and the experience for the employee will not be encouraging. You do not want employees avoiding you because your listening skills are poor and unpleasant.

- Ask the employee. Reverse the same acknowledgement tactic when you are giving a direction or immediately after you have a discussion with an employee, "Tell me what we just decided on?" Or "Please summarize for me what we just discussed?"

Be Proactive. A common issue for the new manager is not acting quickly enough when a problem is starting to be evident. We have known several experienced managers who let problems fester excessively long without addressing them. Take for example the manager who ignores an employee who consistently comes to work late. In this situation the late employee quickly learns there are no consequences from the manager for coming late. In reality, there are consequences. The employee is actually being encouraged. He benefits from the extra time he gets to use, perhaps by staying in his warm bed a little longer, or running a morning errand, or catching a second cup of coffee at his favorite coffee shop. In effect, the manager's lack of action is not only maintaining the problem but likely increasing it. There are also other important consequences for the manager operating in this common example. Most notably, the other employees see that the manager is not facing the situation. The message they learn is the manager does not face up to problems.

The trap the new manager can fall into is thinking they must charge ahead to demonstrate their capability of taking charge and making quick decisions. The best advice for the new manager is to get out ahead of problems or issues that may be starting to surface in the office or with specific employees. However, being proactive in this sense does not mean acting without careful consideration and doing the necessary looking into and fact checking. We have known new managers who did not act quickly enough when faced with a problem, as well as those who acted too quickly without first researching the situation.

The new manager must not be afraid to tackle problems head on but at the same time cannot be seen as making flip or careless actions. Employees should see the new manager being firm, decisive and meeting problems head on but also acting in ways that demonstrate good judgment in knowing the facts and understanding the issues.

Being proactive for the new manager can mean letting the employee know he/she was late twice in the last week and asking for the reasons. If the employee reports a problem outside of the work environment, being proactive can mean making a referral for professional help. At the same time being clear by saying, "I expect you to be here on time from now on," and stating the reasons.

Being proactive for the new manager can mean reviewing an examiner's daily production totals to watch for evidence the employee is falling below the daily standard. Informally meeting with the employee to review the productivity totals and stating what is expected is a proactive way to generate performance.

Being proactive for the new manager can mean holding a team meeting to discuss the fact the office has received several customer complaints about service, and the complaints concern team behavior for which, everyone is responsible.

Solicit Employee Input. We were once asked to work with a new title manager who had a reputation for keeping to herself. She was an excellent technical manager and knew title production like the back of her hand and only recently had been promoted to manager. We interviewed the manager, her supervisor, and a sample of her employees in her office. This is what we learned: each morning she walked through the front door and straight into her office and closed the door. She looked over the order count totals for the day before, checked a report that indicated a need by dates for current orders in the pipeline, checked and responded to her emails and then made calls to specific employees in other offices or to customers, about problems or issues that needed her attention.

She routinely stayed in her office during most of the day and worked on commercial files. Production staff did interrupt her frequently during the day, but she had little time to discuss issues and often just corrected the problem herself as fast as she could. At lunchtime, she often ate in the common area where there were employees present, but seldom looked up from her newspaper. In her staff meetings, she mostly talked at her employees without much dialogue with her staff. Late in the afternoon she re-checked order status in the pipeline and reviewed examiner assignments for new orders that had come in during the day. At closing time, she would make the trek back through the office barely looking up and seldom stopping to talk with employees who were working late.

When we asked the new manager if she had the time to provide feedback or solicit employee input she said she had little or no opportunities to do so. This misunderstanding by the new title manager is not uncommon. Often managers in the title insurance industry, by design, have to accomplish a sizeable amount of production work themselves and believe they have little opportunity for management activities like providing feedback or soliciting input. Of course we viewed the situation differently and worked with the manager to develop new ways to consider her daily schedule. The first thing we did was to stress the importance of providing frequent feedback and soliciting employee input. We then discussed what opportunities she might have given her daily schedule.

This is an example of the plan we developed with the new manager:

1. First thing in the morning, stop as you enter and walk through the office, to speak with one or two employees at their desks. Take this opportunity to comment on the past day's performance. Single out good work for difficult files or handling customer issues. Provide general encouragement and praise as much as you can in these informal moments. Talk with different people each morning.

2. Use a 'Morning Huddle.' This is a brief 10 to 15 minute stand-up in the work-area, informal meeting, where you gather the production staff together in one place and discuss the day's work and any problems or rush orders that are anticipated. Tell your employees you will have the Morning Huddle daily, at the same time, and staff should anticipate ahead of time specific questions they could ask during this time, in lieu of interrupting the manager throughout the day. During the Huddle, provide feedback on work from the previous day and ask employees if there are any questions or problems you can help with or act as a resource for. Provide general encouragement and positively comment on work from the last workday.

3. Use emails to provide supportive encouragement and feedback. Do not only send an email to an employee when there is a problem. For example, use email feedback to an examiner as a way to point out to the commitment total for the previous day was excellent.

4. When employees come to you with a problem, remind them to try to anticipate questions to ask during the Morning Huddle. For problems or issues that need immediate attention, ask the employees first, what they think should be done first. Provide positive and constructive feedback on the answers they provide and make suggestions on what they might additionally do.

5. When you eat lunch in the common area, use the time to talk and interact with employees on an informal basis. Ask them how they are doing. Ask them about the files they are working on. Ask them about the customers they have talked with during the morning. Provide feedback and encouragement on what people say.

6. Use your lunch time differently. Take someone out to lunch to discuss an issue or provide constructive feedback. Invite an employee into your office to share a lunch with you and use the opportunity to provide feedback to the employee. Consider ordering pizza for the office on Fridays for a week's work well done. Use the informal time for additional feedback.

7. During your staff meetings make it a habit to ask for employee input. Find out what they are thinking and ask them for their ideas. Ask them how they think the office is functioning. What are their ideas for improvement? What feedback can they give you on things you might do differently as a manager to improve office functioning? Use each meeting as an opportunity to point out several positives and encourage your team as a whole. If you know you have specific employees who like public acknowledgement for tasks well done, look for opportunities in your meeting to provide specific acknowledgement.

8. At the end of the day, as you exit the office, stop and talk with employees about the day and what is coming up. Use this time to listen.

Delegate Tasks. One of the difficult issues for a new manager is stepping in to complete tasks when the work should more appropriately be completed by an employee or team. The tendency is to want to make sure the work is correct or done promptly, so the new manager does the work himself, rather than delegating it to someone whose role it should be. It is a natural tendency, the new manager wants to make sure that nothing wrong happens on his new watch and ends up over-compensating, trying to do too many things himself. The term micro managing is often used to describe managers who do tasks that they should leave or delegate to others. We often hear these managers say something like "I would rather do it myself, that way I know it will be done right."

There are two main problems with this approach. First, a manager's ultimate role is to help others do the work. In this role, the manager acts as a facilitator and resource provider. When managers take over the work themselves, they are not helping their employees grow and develop. Secondly, most managers who have difficulty delegating over-extend themselves in terms of time. They do not accomplish in total all that they need to as managers because they are doing work that others should be doing. Here are a few tips to consider:

1. Ask what they think. When an employee comes to you with a question about a task do not simply give them the answer and send them on their way. Ask them what they think the answer should be. If they give you the right answer praise their response. If they give you a partially correct answer praise the correct part and provide constructive feedback on the part that needs to be corrected. If you follow these steps you will be increasing the probability your employees are learning and will not have to come to you as frequently in the future.

2. Who can do this? Before taking on a new task, ask the question: Is there anyone else that is capable, better positioned, or should be doing this job? If the answer is yes, consider delegating the task.

3. Make a list of all your responsibilities and the current tasks you do. Make a second list of the employees you supervise and work with. Put the two lists side by side. Go through your first list item by item while looking at the second list and ask the question: Is there anyone else that is capable, better positioned, or should be doing this task? If the answer is yes, consider delegating the task.

4. Walk away. Leave your office for a day and determine how the office or team can work without you. Repeat the experiment by

being gone two, three, and five days. If they can effectively work without you, you are doing a good job of managing.

Be Careful of Friendships. This is a potentially dangerous pitfall for the new manager, especially in those cases where the new manager has been promoted and now is having to supervise employees that were once peers. There is also the danger the new manager will use friendship as a tactic to impress employees or win them over.

We knew a new manager who fell into this trap. She was an excellent closer who had been promoted to the head of the escrow department because of her technical expertise and because of her ability to work well with different types of people. As a closer, she frequently went out to lunch with the other closers and processors; she attended social events with them on weekends, socialized often in smaller groups after work and counted two of her peers as close personal friends. When she was promoted she did little to change her social patterns. When it came time to discipline one of her previous friends, she failed to convince the majority of the staff in her office that she was being fair. She later told us it took quite a long time for her to re-develop trust among her employees and she had learned a valuable lesson.

The new manager must be aware they cannot appear to be playing favorites in any way with employees they worked alongside of once. This is not to say that the new manager cannot be friendly and social with past friends, but they must also know that it is important to draw a clear line of demarcation. That line must clearly designate that the new manager will be treating everyone in the same professional way with no exceptions for past friendships.

The new manager must also understand that at some point she will be making professional management decisions with each of the employees she supervises. In making those decisions, the new manager must be fair, honest and take the situation and other variables into consideration. Friendship cannot be one of the variables considered.

Understand the Big Picture. The new manager to be successful must take into account the bigger picture. An office is a system with many moving parts. These parts include procedures, communications, management, schedules, workflow, software and hardware technology, space utilization and employee skills and abilities, to name a few. To clearly understand and manage how the system functions the manager must consider not only the integration of all its moving parts, but often, the context in which the system operates within the larger company as a whole.

The tendency for the new manager is to focus attention exclusively on the one part that is immediately confronting or affecting her without taking the larger system or context into consideration. This means for example, if a change in software is anticipated, workflow, daily procedures, and the skill levels of specific employees need to be considered in planning for the software change within the team or unit. It may also mean the manager needs to take into consideration how the software changes will effect workflow either originating from other offices or that will be passed onto the other offices or units of the company.

A manager once complained to us that one of his most experienced examiners was being re-assigned to a larger centralized production unit within the company. The manager said he was exasperated and could not figure how to explain the change to the other employees in his office. Later in discussing the incident with the manager's supervisor we learned that the manager had immediately complained about how the change would affect his office, and without any further investigation, had taken his complaints directly to the company owner. However, here is the critical piece, the supervisor also told us that commitment turn-time throughout the company was suffering, customers were complaining throughout the region and an experienced examiner was needed for training purposes. Clearly, the manager had not understood or considered the bigger picture.

One idea to understand your operation and see the larger picture is to make a list of all the system components that operate in your team, unit, or office. When you anticipate a change or major decision, make sure you have taken into consideration each of your system components. If you operate in a larger company with several offices or units, always consider your actions in the larger systems context.

Manage Up. One piece of advice we always give a manager is to 'Manage Up.' Managing up can mean asking your supervisor what types of information she needs on a weekly\monthly basis to do her job better. Managing up means pushing information to your supervisor to help keep him/her informed. For example, do not let your supervisor be the last person to find out that a problem exists. Let your supervisor know that an issue or problem may be on the horizon. When you provide your supervisor with information ahead of time about a possible problem, she/he is not caught off guard and is in a better position to consider possible actions of a preventive nature.

When you manage up you proactively work with your supervisor by acting as a resource for her. For example, try initiating assistance or volunteering to work on certain projects. In essence, you are helping smooth the management path between you and your supervisor as well as providing assistance in other ways. For the new manager, managing up can mean understanding your supervisor's management style. You may need to adjust your style to fit hers, to improve communications and joint decision-making.

Managing up can mean pointing out growing trends in performance reports. For example, with order counts increasing or decreasing, the consequences anticipated in the workflow pipeline for title and escrow production. Managing up can mean helping your supervisor frame company issues, making suggestions for improving communications.

Understand the Facts. One of the tough lessons for a new manager is understanding that employees do not always have all the facts or information to form the right perception. Sometimes information is confidential and cannot be communicated. Such is often the case with personnel issues. At other times, employees simply do not have all the information they need to form the correct conclusion. In effect, the perceptions that employees form may be incorrect or partially incorrect, but those perceptions are what the manager must be aware of and manage to.

For example, Chris knows that the first perception other people have of him is that he is somewhat reserved, quiet, and analytical. The facts are those tendencies are true, but he also has another more personable side that is outgoing and very social, that people often do not get to see. Through the years he has learned that to be successful in working with people, he has to counteract the perception people easily form. He often has to go out of his way to show people his other side. In other words, Chris has learned he must manage his behavior by purposefully showing his personable side.

Managers are often faced with the same type of dilemma. Employees have a perception that is incorrect and needs to change. The facts may point to something different, but it is the perception the manager must understand and manage.

When we interview employees and managers in title insurance companies and ask the question: "What do your customers think about your customer service?" The typical answer is that the service is good or very good. However, if we measure commitment turn-time data, or conduct customer satisfaction surveys, we sometimes find a different story. Commitment turn-time is often slower than market standards, customer satisfaction scores are average at best and a majority of orders comes from too small of a customer base. Essentially, what we find out is the customers' perceptions do not match the employees or owners' perception.

If employees believe the service they are providing is 'good' they have little reason to change their behavior. Why should they, their perception is they are doing what is necessary. To improve customer service managers must understand the customers' perception, as well as the employees and they must work to improve service and align perceptions.

Guiding Principle

> **Managers must understand the facts and manage perceptions**

Managing Younger Workers

There has been quite a bit written about the difference in the workforce among generations of workers and it is true that there are differences of which managers should be aware. For the new manager, understanding these differences can be useful in establishing a good working relationship with both older and younger employees.
As you probably understand by now, we do not advocate a one-style-fits-all approach to management. Every management situation brings with it different variables to take into consideration and the behavioral tendencies of both managers and employees are important to consider. We advocate that managers should consider adjusting their style to fit the management situation they are faced with. It then naturally follows, we also recommend that the manager take into account possible generational differences. However, remember, everyone is different and you cannot rely on stereotypes. There have been several negative characteristics pointed out about the younger worker, but what we think is important is to understand and leverage the younger worker's strengths. Here is a short list to consider about younger workers:

1. They tend to be more educated. They have had more opportunities to receive education compared to their parents and grandparents.

2. They are technologically oriented. They grew up with computers from day one and continue to integrate the latest technology into everything they do.

3. They are not easily impressed by authority. One good way to win their respect is through results. They value and respect competence.

4. They want to be a part of the decision making process. Their parents have asked for their input, their teachers have asked for their input, they expect their managers to ask for their input.

5. They are self-reliant. More was expected of them earlier in life. Each generation has had to face their own set of challenges, but with each generation the level of expectation rises. The younger generation has been given more tools and has received more education to be more self-reliant, earlier in life.

6. They are skeptical. This is a good thing. We want our employees to challenge our thinking constructively.

7. They expect a balance between work and their own personal lives. They expect their employer to understand this.

8. They will look to advance and change positions. The average young worker will move in and out of at least six different positions or companies by the time they are 30 years old.

Managing Older Workers

This topic is relatively easy for us to talk about since we represent this group. However, there are some tendencies to understand about the older worker that will help the new manager. Our first recommendation is obvious; since older workers have been around for a while, they do have quite a bit of experience and knowledge to draw from. Think of them as libraries to turn to as resources. They will appreciate that you acknowledge their experience and turn to them for advice or as mentors. Listening well to what they have to say is another important key. The older worker will look to see if the new manager is patient and thoughtful and does not rush to make impulsive decisions.

New managers do not need to be overly concerned about the older worker understanding the management chain. Since they grew up in work environments where emphasis was placed on hierarchy, they know you are the boss and will likely respect that. Many older workers in fact have been managers at one time themselves so they are in a good position to understand some of the management issues the new manager is facing.

Communication is an important variable to consider. The older worker may not be as adept or use the communication methods a younger manager might favor. Chris's daughters text what they want to communicate, about 90 percent of the time! With the older worker, do not assume what modes of communication will work the best, find out and then proceed.

Take age ranges into consideration. There are differences to consider between, for example, a 40-year-old worker and someone who is 60 years old. Their goals will be different, what is rewarding for them will likely be different, and their needs will be different. The task of the new manager is to understand there will be differences and then discover what they are. Below is a table that compares additional tendencies at work among two older generations and younger workers:

TENDENCIES AT WORK	BORN <1946	"BOOMERS"	YOUNGER WORKERS
OUTLOOK	Practical	Optimistic	Skeptical
WORK ETHIC	Dedicated	Driven	Balanced
AUTHORITY	Respectful	Love\Hate	Unimpressed
LEADERSHIP	Hierarchy	Consensus	Competence
PERSEPCTIVE	Civic-minded	Team-Focus	Self-reliant

Guiding Principle

> *Understanding the differences among generations in the workforce is a key to establishing good working relationships with both younger and older workers.*

Managing Your Time

New managers are faced with many responsibilities they are experiencing for the first time. Many managers find the transition difficult because they have not had to juggle or handle a diverse set of roles or responsibilities in the past. We have found time management is often stated as a problem, but seldom do managers have a specific set of steps to follow to make improvements. If time management is an issue for you, consider the following steps:

1. Start by making a list of the activities you engage in throughout the month. Some of these activities will occur daily, some weekly and some only once a month. Divide a sheet of paper into three columns and as each day passes continue to list your activities until you have a good representation of your total activity for one month. As you make your lists indicate the amount of time you typically spend on each activity. Some of the activities you list will be one-time events, but the majority will likely be activities that you repeat either weekly or monthly.

2. After you have completed your general activity list, start your time management planning on a Monday morning. Review your completed general activity list and insert on a calendar the daily and weekly activities you will plan for the week ahead. Insert your activities into time blocks on your calendar. For example, conducts morning huddle from 9:00 a.m. to 9:15 a.m. Answers emails 9:15 to 9:45 a.m.; 12:30 p.m. to 1:00 p.m. and 4:30 to 5:00 p.m., and so on. To the extent possible, look ahead on your monthly calendar and set dates and times for activities, as far ahead as possible.

3. At the end of each day, evaluate how well you have adhered to your daily time management schedule and make adjustments on your calendar for the next day. Record the actual amount of time you spent on specific activities versus the amount of time that you have planned.

4. As the week progresses, make changes to your planned days based on your performance to date.

5. As the weeks progress, identify additional activities you did not anticipate or did not consider and add them to your general activity list.

6. On Monday of each week, evaluate your past weeks' time management and make adjustments for the week ahead.

7. After a month of planning and tracking your time, evaluate how well you have done. Based on your actual time usage, determine which activities were the biggest users of your time. You can assign percentages to get a clearer picture of which activities are taking the greatest amount of your time.

8. Develop goals for how you would like to change or improve your time usage for the next month. For example, I spent 20 percent (i.e., 90 minutes per day) of my time answering emails. My goal for the next month is to decrease my email percentage to 13 percent (i.e., 60 minutes per day).

9. Repeat the above process (steps 2-8) for the next month.

10. Each month continue to monitor how close you come to your time usage goals and determine what you need to adjust.

There is a tendency for the new manager to work on the most immediate issue or task that presents itself, on any given day, instead of stepping back and planning, in a more purposeful way, how available time will be best utilized. We always tell new managers: "You need to control time instead of having time control you!"

There are many advantages to using an electronic calendar on a computer or smart phone. However, sometimes in starting time management, an old-fashioned manual list, one that you write and scribble on, will work best.

Here is an example of a time management plan for an escrow manager. The number in parentheses is minutes for the task.

ESCROW MANAGER ACTIVITY LIST		
DAILY	WEEKLY	MONTHLY
Conduct morning huddle (15)	Review performance numbers (15)	Plan agenda for Escrow Team meeting (30)
Review closing figures (30)	Complete H.R. activities (60)	Hold Escrow Team meeting (45)
Conduct morning closing (60)	Check staff schedules (30)	Attend manager meetings (90)
Answer email (60)	Meet with sales staff (60)	Review performance numbers (30)
Return\answer\makes telephone calls (30-45)	Work on planning assignments from supervisor (60-120)	Review budget (30)
Answers staff questions (60)	Meet with customers (120)	Review P&L (30)
Reviews closings for next day (60)	Attend customer events (90)	Conduct performance reviews (60)
Review new processing files (30)	Meet with staff individually for supervision purposes (60)	Meet with supervisor (60)

TAKE AWAY ACTIVITY
CHAPTER 8
STARTING TO MANAGE

1. Copy this table or use a calendar.

2. Use the table (or a calendar) to record your activities for a week.

3. Identify those activities that are most important or priorities.

4. Identify those activities that someone else should do.

5. Identify those activities that should be moved to a different time.

6. Plan your time for next week (write in your schedule) and record your actual activities that week. Repeat the process for a month.

Time	Monday	Tuesday	Wednesday	Thursday	Friday
8:00					
8:30					
9:00					
9:30					
10:00					
10:30					
11:00					
11:30					
12:00					
12:30					
1:00					
1:30					
2:00					
2:30					
3:00					
3:30					
4:00					
4:30					
5:00					
5:30					
6:00					

GUIDING PRINCIPLES
CHAPTER 8
STARTING TO MANAGE

1. Acquiring technical knowledge and skills seldom prepare an employee to manage successfully.

2. It is important for the new manager to have a plan for the first day, the first week, month and quarter.

3. The demonstration of short-term gains, improvements and success is critical for the new manager in the first 90 days.

4. If managers know and understand their behavior tendencies, they can be in a better position to adjust them when needed.

5. There are several tactics new managers should consider to gain and build trust:

    a. Be honest, direct and follow-through.

    b. Be accessible.

    c. Listen well.

    d. Be proactive.

    e. Solicit employee input and feedback.

    f. Delegate tasks.

    g. Be careful of friendships.

    h. Understand the big picture.

    i. Manage up.

    j. Manage your time.

6. Managers must understand the facts and manage perceptions.

7. Understanding the differences among generations in the workforce is a key to establishing good working relationships with both younger and older workers.

CHAPTER 9

INFLUENCING BEHAVIOR

Employees often think managers speak another language, a language they cannot understand. Consider the three statements below. In each, the manager is complaining about an employee's behavior without being clear what he wants the employee to do differently.

- Jane has a bad attitude.
- Jim is not a good team player.
- Sally never takes any initiative.

The problem with these statements is that they are vague and open to several interpretations. In these examples, it is likely the employee believes the manager means one thing while the manager believes he has indicated something entirely different. In our experience, simply telling an employee what he/she is doing wrong accomplishes very little other than to create anger and animosity. If you want a person to behave differently, you first have to tell the person specifically what you want him/her to do. For example:

- Jane, you need to smile and say, "Hello, how may I help you?" when customers enter.
- Jim, you need to volunteer to help others in meetings.
- Sally, you need to go to your supervisor when you have a problem on a file you cannot fix.

Telling employees how they need to behave in a specific way is the first step in changing or improving employee behavior. However, to be effective, managers also need to create a connection between telling and doing. What we mean is that managers need to make sure that desired behavior is encouraged, supported, and rewarded.

In Chapter 9, we start by discussing the process of pinpointing behavior. Next, we discuss what behavioral psychologists refer to as the ABC's. The acronym refers to antecedents, behavior and consequences. In our view, using the ABC's is one way a manager can effectively create a connection between telling and doing.

Pinpointing Behavior

Managers often ask us "How specific do we need to be when explaining what behavior we expect?" Here are four rules to follow to ensure you are being specific. We call this method pinpointing. Pinpoints are observable. We can directly see or hear the pinpointed behavior. The main rule for pinpointing behavior is the behavior you identified is an observable action, an action two or more people can reliably agree they have seen or heard.

Guiding Principle

We pinpoint to make sure we are specific with our employees.

For example, the statement "Bob is a good team player," can be made more specific by focusing on pinpointing what we mean by team player. In each example below, we make our statements more specific by pinpointing behaviors we can see (volunteering and asking).

- Bob is a good team player, when he volunteers for team projects.
- Bob is a good team player, when he asks team members if he can help.

Pinpoints are measurable. Notice in the paired examples below, the second statement improves on the first statement by adding a measurable pinpoint. In these examples, the pinpoint includes units and time.

- Nancy is very productive.
- Nancy is very productive; she completes ten searches a day.
- Sam has a good level of customer coverage.

- Sam has a good level of customer coverage; he averages four customer lunches, ten office visits, and one customer presentation a week.

Pinpoints provide multiple exemplars. Some employee behavior is best described by providing several pinpoints. Note how the following description is improved in the second statement by adding several observable pinpoints.

- Jerry is an enthusiastic closer.
- Jerry is an enthusiastic closer; he smiles when customers approach, he gets out from behind his desk and shakes each person's hand, he uses optimistic words like "Yes," "Of course," "Certainly," and people laugh and smile in his closings.

Pinpoints identify behaviors and outcomes that collectively help define the employee behavior we want. If some employee behavior is best pinpointed by giving several examples, other employee behavior is best pinpointed by identifying multiple outcomes occurring in different situations. Note how the example below is improved in the second statement by adding several pinpoints that occur at different times.

1. Tom is a good salesperson.
2. Tom is a good salesman:
- He returns all customer phone calls within two hours
- He submits Sales call reports on time
- He completes two office visits a day.
- He has four customer lunches a week.
- He makes five customer presentations a month.

In talking to employees about their performance, if we pinpoint results or behaviors that are specific, observable, measurable, and defined by multiple examples we eliminate the possibilities for any employee confusion.

Think of an employee who needs to improve in some way. Now take a moment and write down the behavior pinpoints you would use with this employee to state clearly, what you expect.

Connecting telling and doing

Each day at work, there are multiple opportunities and ways for a manager to influence employee behavior. For example, we can show the employee what we want, we can personally tell the employee, we can send emails, we might provide checklists, we can list out procedures step by step, and we can hold meetings. Behavioral scientists call these management actions "antecedents," meaning they occur before the behavior we want. Antecedents are prompts, reminders, or signals that tell us it is time to behave. In the best examples, antecedents are like triggers, they influence behavior immediately.

Guiding Principle

> **Antecedents are actions to prompt or "trigger" the behavior we want or expect.**

As managers, we want these antecedent prompts to influence our employees to behave in certain ways. When we hold a meeting to discuss improving customer service, we expect that the discussion about what needs to be done will cause employees to provide better customer service. When we remind an employee to use a quality checklist, we expect that our reminder will cause the employee to follow and use the checklist. When we send an email to an employee, we expect the employee to read the email and follow our instructions.

In our daily lives, antecedent signals are all around us. In the morning the alarm clock rings and reminds us to wake up and get going. We read the newspaper to find out the daily weather to determine what clothing to wear. When we are driving and see a 45 mile per hour speed limit sign, we slow down. All of these events are examples of antecedents, signals that prompt a person to behave.

Unfortunately, research shows us that antecedents alone are not always effective in producing behavior. For example, when the alarm clock rings some of us turn over and go back to sleep. This is why the snooze alarm was invented.

When Roger was in graduate school, he kept missing his morning class because he would turn off the alarm. Finally, in desperation, he hired a friend to call him every morning. She would call at 6:45 and if Roger did not call her back at 7:00 she would call again. Answering the phone forced him out of bed and once he was up, he would stay up. Now with the advent of the iPhone and the clock app, Roger sets three alarms on his iPhone, one at 6:00 am, one at 6:30 am and one at 6:45 am. In addition, he places his iPhone away from his bed, so he has to get up and out of bed to turn it off. By the final alarm, he is always awake and up. His iPhone is doing the same thing the friend did by calling, it is triggering action and it keeps prompting the action until the behavior occurs.

Guiding Principle

> **Antecedents alone are not always effective in producing behavior.**

Research on antecedent control reveals that signals are most effective if they are associated with positive consequences when the desired behavior occurs. For example, a manager sends an email out to five employees reminding each person to bring a copy of a report to the noon meeting. At the meeting, two employees show up on time and have a copy of the report. However, one employee does not show up and has to be called to the meeting because he never opened up the email, and two of the employees did not read through the email so they arrive at the meeting without the report.

Guiding Principle

> **Antecedents are most effective if they are associated with consequences for employee behavior.**

This is a critical moment in every managers work life. Two employees responded correctly, they paid attention to the manager's instructions and three employees did not respond correctly. So what should the manager do? Some managers will 1) delay the meeting until the missing employee can be found and other managers will 2) bring extra copies of the report, knowing no one reads their email, so they can hand out the report at the meeting.

Taking a step back, we can see that Option 1 and Option 2 sends the message that employees do not need to read or comply with the manager's emails. Suppose instead the manager started the meeting without the missing employee and sent the two without reports back to their office to get their reports while the meeting continued without them. Now the message is read my emails or else. In this example, the consequence for reading and complying with the managers instructions (email) is positive and the consequence for not following the manager's instruction is negative.

When the employee ignores the email from the manager and nothing happened, he was more likely to ignore the next message. If Roger could turn his iPhone alarm off from bed, the consequences of staying in a warm bed might be stronger than being late. However, placing the iPhone alarm on the dresser across the room, forces Roger to get out of bed, and once out, he starts his day. In each example, the antecedent (prompt) is only effective when the behavior we want occurs and is reinforced.

We cannot emphasize this point enough. Providing positive consequences for the behavior we want occurring following a prompt is the most effective action a manager can do to change and improve the behavior of employees. Providing positive consequences in a timely fashion after the behavior you are seeking will increase the probability that the behavior will continue to occur in the future. In fact, the very best solution for a manager is to provide effective clear antecedents followed up by positive consequences once the employee behaves.

| Antecedent ⇨ Behavior ⇦ Positive Consequence |

Before we go too far it is very important to understand that consequences can be both positive and negative, rewarding (reinforcing) and punishing. Research shows that in most workplaces there are very few positive consequences and far too many negative consequences.

Guiding Principle

In most workplaces, there are very few positive consequences and far too many negative consequences.

In Table 6 we provide examples of antecedents, behavior, and consequences at work. Antecedents and consequences occur in the workplace all the time. In Table 6 look at the **Behavior** column first and then for each Behavior, examine the **Antecedent** that prompts or triggers the behavior and the **Consequence** that follows and reinforces the behavior.

Table 6. Examples of Antecedent, Behavior, and Consequence.

ANTECEDENT	BEHAVIOR	CONSEQUENCE
Co-worker says, "Can someone help?"	Sally offers to help.	Co-worker says "thank you." Manager says "thanks."
Jane receives training on how to greet customers when they enter office.	Jane greets customers in the reception area with "Hello, how may I help you?"	The manager observes Jane and provides positive feedback as soon as possible.
Manager meets with Jim to discuss ways to become a better team player.	Jim volunteers at a staff meeting to help with a new project.	Manager thanks Jim in meeting for volunteering and sends him a thank you note.
Sales Managers tells Account Rep. that Sales Plan is due at end of month and sends weekly reminders.	Account Representatives submits sales plan on time.	Manager provides feedback about the plan being on time and the quality of the final draft.
Title Production Manager sets productivity standard of 8 exams per day.	Examiner averages 10 residential exams per day for the month.	Manager surprises Examiner with extra day off for job well done.
Manager asks Bob to come to work on time.	Bob comes to work on time.	Manager praises Bob for being on time each day he is early.

In the examples so far, the antecedents are reminders, prompts, notes, all designed to cause an appropriate behavior. When the behavior occurs, the behavior is followed by praise, attention, or some other form of positive consequence or positive reinforcement. Before we leave the topic of consequences, we have to acknowledge the fact that the consequences can be misused or misapplied. For example, sometimes, positive consequences can reward negative behavior.

Likewise, sometimes the absence of any negative consequences following inappropriate behavior will signal that it is alright to misbehave. Consider the example of the male employee who is always saying rude comments and making fun of one co-worker to other staff. Such behavior is clearly inappropriate, but it occurs/continues because of the reaction of the coworkers. If they laugh and encourage his rude comments (positive consequences) he will continue to make rude remarks. If on the other hand, coworkers ignored his rude remarks, or even walked away from him when he was rude, he would likely stop making such remarks.

For a manager to be effective in the workplace, he/she must understand how antecedents and consequences, present in the workplace, influence employee behavior. In addition, the manager has to be aware how events that happen outside of work, can affect employee behavior at work. Often times, events that are happening outside of work cause behavior problems at work.

Guiding Principle

> ### *Managers must understand how antecedents and consequences influence employee behavior.*

For example, a female employee has a fight with her husband and daughter before coming to work. The fight at home involved yelling, screaming, and considerable crying. Such emotional events are not easy to forget and our bodies and brains often take a long time to get over such emotions. Even though the employee is at work and her husband and daughter are not present, she may continue to think about what happened and continue to experience the physiological effect of the earlier events. Now when a co-worker complains about a file or when a customer becomes difficult, the employee reacts with unexpected and inappropriate anger.

In this example, an event that is no longer present is triggering inappropriate behavior because we are still feeling or thinking about the event. Psychologists call such antecedents, **Setting Events** because they set the stage for later behavior.

In all likelihood, what is happening to the employee is the emotion and remembering the earlier events are still present, but from a coworkers or customers' point of view, the inappropriate behavior appears to have come out of nowhere with no clear antecedent.

Setting events can trigger both positive and negative behaviors. In the prior example, we have an argument and it influences us for the rest of the day. Turn this situation around. What happens when a customer complements you for delivering great service? Hopefully, you feel good long after the customer is gone. Setting Event.

Guiding Principle

Events that continue to trigger behavior after they are gone are called Setting Events

Positive Consequences

If we want employee behavior to improve, we have to arrange antecedents and setting events and we have to ensure there are positive consequences (praise and words of encouragement) for the behavior. As a manager, you have to find ways to observe behavior and provide positive consequences when the behavior you want actually happens. The more immediate the consequence the more effective the consequence. Each day, there are many opportunities available to praise performance. We consider creating a situation where you can reinforce employees on a daily basis an example of Supportive Coaching.

In order to be a supportive coach, the manager must understand what the positive consequences are for the employee in question. Remember, what is rewarding for one person may not be for another. Popeye loved spinach, but not everyone does. We all have different likes and dislikes and what some people find rewarding or reinforcing, another person may find unrewarding or even punishing. For example, some employees will enjoy and benefit from public praise and encouragement while others will prefer that their manager talk to them and encourage or praise them in private. For some employees verbal praise may not be important, but written encouragement and positive feedback in the form of an email will be reinforcing. Even something as obvious as money may only work for some people and not others. For some employees a word of praise once a week is far more valuable than a small bonus at the end of the year. In order to be a supportive coach, a manager needs to be aware and observe how employees are reacting to the consequences the manager is providing.

Guiding Principle

> ### *In order for employees to improve and change, they need positive consequences for their behavior.*

Managers should actively look for opportunities daily to praise and reinforce behavior. One of the nice things about positive consequences is most are easy to do. Suppose an employee stays late and finishes work on a file for the morning. A manager could provide any of the positive consequences on the following list. Review the list with one of your employees in mind and decide if the employee in question would view the consequence listed as positive?

1. Walk to the employee's desk and praise the behavior ('thank you').
2. Bring the employee a drink (e.g., cup of coffee) to start the day.
3. Send an email thanking the employee with a copy to the team and owners.
4. Send a hand written thank you note.
5. Buy the employee a morning snack (donuts) or lunch.
6. Take the employee to lunch.
7. Recognize the employee's efforts in a staff meeting.
8. Give an employee early leave for working late.
9. Write a personal letter of merit for the employee's file.
10. Arrange for the president of the company to thank the employee.
11. Give the employee a bonus or gift in recognition.

Notice in the list of positive consequences, how the level of personal involvement on the part of the manager or others increases with each level of consequence. Most of the time, the size or level of consequence should match the behavior in question. The employee stayed 10 minutes to finish a file, the manager says 'thanks,' and nothing more. The employee stays late an hour, deserves 'thanks and a donut.' The employee works late every night this week, deserves a letter in his file. Over rewarding is never a good idea, because it creates false expectations. However, remember, behavior can never be praised enough.

Punishment and Negative Consequences

We worked in a title office once where the office manager had a reputation for yelling and screaming at employees almost daily. He would yell about customer service needing to be better, he would complain about order counts, he would demean employees for their poor performance. He even had a microphone outside his office connected to the PA system, and he would make announcements over the public address system where he would yell at, criticize, or complain about, a specific employee.

When we asked the employees about his behavior they said that it had been going on like that for several years. Many people said the manager was a "lion with no teeth," and later he would apologize and give out "I'm sorry" gifts. However, when we questioned staff further, we found out employees tended to keep their heads down when the manager was present and in one of his "moods." Likewise, we learned that employees did not go into the manager's office or ask the manager a question unless they had to. In essence, staff tried to do very little around the manager other than trying to look busy and keep out of sight. They were afraid to do anything, for fear of receiving the wrath of the manager. Employees did not talk to the manager, they did not volunteer or initiate information, they did not dare to try anything new, in fact, they did only what they were told and got out of the office as quickly as possible each day.

We have observed this pattern more than once, and while we believe this management style is completely inappropriate in business, we know that such rough management can get immediate results. However, in the end, the company had high turnover, the people who stayed were employees who stayed at the company because they had no alternatives. We like to say, managers who use fear and punishing consequences are trying to get results the wrong way.

Guiding Principle

Managers who use fear and punishing consequences are trying to get results the wrong way.

There may be some situations where negative consequences (punishment) may be appropriate for a manager to use. For example, if an employee shows up dressed inappropriately, sending the person home to change and docking her pay for the time missed may serve to punish not following the dress code of a company. However, the use of threats, criticism, and forms of restrictions, while a common tactic in military training, are inappropriate at work.

For example, if an Escrow Assistant makes calculation mistakes, the Escrow Officer could use criticism, but this tactic never corrects a mistake. Likewise, the Escrow Officer could announce that she is taking over the files and working them up herself, but this action only teaches the assistant that making mistakes result in less work. In most cases, the repeated use of punishment and negative consequences by a manager will result in avoidance behavior, underachievement, and poor performance on the part of employees. Ideally, we want employees engaging in productive work because of positive consequences and not because of fear of punishment.

Look for Opportunities to manage the ABC's

Managers, to be effective need to look actively for opportunities to provide clear antecedents and consequences for specific employee behavior. The truth is that in the natural environment of the workplace, employee behavior, antecedents and consequences are occurring all the time, regardless of whether the manager is present or not.

Guiding Principle

> *Managers should create opportunities to provide daily antecedents and consequences for employee behavior.*

In the following example, see if you can identify the antecedents and consequences that are controlling employee behavior.

Sally is the first to arrive at the office in the morning, sees the security panel on the front door and enters the code. The panel beeps and she enters as the door lock is released. Inside, she quickly moves to her desk where she sees her empty coffee cup sitting by the side of her computer. She immediately decides to go and make coffee in the office kitchen. A few minutes later, while she is enjoying the first sips of her freshly made coffee, she hears a phone ringing and rushes to a nearby phone to take the call. It is the office manager on the phone asking Sally if she will get an order started that came in late the night before. Sally starts entering the new order into the company's web-based system and quickly receives confirmation from the software that all the correct customer information has been added, a confirmation has been sent to the customer and the order has been routed to title production. A half hour later, the office manager walks through the door and goes immediately to Sally's desk. The manager asks Sally about the status of the new order and then seconds later, hearing Sally's report, compliments her for her speed and efficiency. Sally lights up with a big smile and says, "Thanks, I really appreciate that!" In turn, the Manager smiles and walks off happy. Later in her office, the manager makes a note to find ways to praise Sally more in the future.

Sally's manager decided to praise Sally for her early morning efforts. In doing so, because Sally appreciated the praise she received, the manager has increased the probability that in the future Sally will act promptly and efficiently. This is a simple example, but it demonstrates how a manager can connect telling and doing. See if you correctly identified the ABC's in our example:

Antecedent	Behavior	Consequence
Sally sees security panel	Enters code	Panel beeps, Sally enters
Sees empty coffee cup	Makes coffee	Enjoys first sips
Phone rings	Picks up phone	Manager is on line
Manager makes request	Sally starts order	Computer provides feedback
Manager checks status	Sally reports status	Sally receives praise

Note that in the above example, consequences can also further act as antecedents for additional behavior. Sally thanked her manager for complimenting her on her speed and efficiency. Sally's "thank you" acted as a trigger for the manager to observe, smile, and take note of the incident. In the future, it will be more likely the manager praises Sally again for similar behavior.

In this chapter, we have considered three ways to influence behavior at work. The first is to be clear about the behavior that is expected. For this, we use a pinpoint. If necessary, we create prompts or reminders, antecedents and setting events that trigger the behavior we want. Finally, when the desired behavior occurs, we have to remember to praise and arrange positive consequences for the behavior.

TAKE AWAY ACTIVITY
CHAPTER 9
INFLUENCING BEHAVIOR

1. Take a moment to think back on the most recent morning in your office or with your team. Identify several positive behaviors that you saw occurring. For each behavior,

   A. Identify a possible antecedent,

   B. Pinpoint the behavior, and

   C. Identify a potential positive consequence.

2. Now identify several positive behaviors that you would like to see but did not see this morning. For each behavior,

   A. Identify a possible antecedent,

   B. Pinpoint the behavior, and

   C. Identify a potential positive consequence.

3. Tomorrow when you perform your morning and afternoon walk around, look for opportunities to prompt and praise.

4. Make a comprehensive list of the positive consequences you might provide to your employees. Remember, positive consequences do not have to be tangible, often times simple praise and encouragement goes a long way.

GUIDING PRINCIPLES
CHAPTER 9
INFLUENCING BEHAVIOR

1. We use behavior pinpoints to make sure we are clear and specific with our employees.

2. Antecedents are actions managers can take to prompt or "trigger" the behavior we want or expect.

3. Antecedents alone are not always effective in producing employee behavior.

4. The antecedents that managers use are most effective if they are associated with consequences for employee behavior.

5. In the workplace, there are very few positive consequences and far too many negative consequences.

6. Managers must understand how antecedents and consequences, present in the workplace, influence employee behavior.

7. In order for employees to improve and change, they need positive consequences for their behavior.

8. Managers who use fear and punishing consequences are trying to get results the wrong way.

9. Managers should actively look for opportunities daily to provide antecedents and consequences for employee behavior.

CHAPTER 10

SETTING EXPECTATIONS

In our experience, effective managers make job and performance expectations clear (antecedents), and use positive consequences when employees act in ways we desire. For a company to be highly successful, each employee must be able to perform his/her specific duties consistently and to a high standard of performance. If you think about your business as a car driving down the highway, the owners and managers may steer the car, but the employees are the engine, transmission, and wheels. If the engine is tuned and running on all cylinders, the car can drive as fast as the road or the law allow. However, if only one cylinder is under performing, the car will not be able to perform at its best.

It sounds rather simple to say that employees are expected to perform their job to certain standards and behave according to company policies, the problem is that people do not do what they are told all the time, and often managers are not sufficiently specific when they try to tell employees what to do. In our experiences, clearly communicating expectations is an essential part of effective management.

In Chapter 10, we discuss two methods for setting expectations with employees: setting goals and objectives and developing performance standards. At the end of the chapter, we examine different ways to communicate expectations to individual employees and to teams. However, before we go any further, let us emphasize again that clear antecedents like goals, objectives and standards will always be more effective when we follow employee behavior and performance with positive consequences and feedback.

Making job expectations specific

When recruiting a new employee, a good company will provide a written job description that lists job roles and responsibilities. When an employee is hired we add to his/her job expectations by explaining company policies and behavioral expectations. After a new employee orientation, most employees have a period of time when they can observe and learn on the job. In our experience, actual on-the-job training is relatively brief, if the new employee has worked in the industry already. Experienced employees are thrown in and either sink or swim.

Fortunately, the majority of title employees are steady, careful, conscientious people who follow rules and require little or no management. For these employees, policy statements, written job descriptions, and a period of questions and answers are sufficient for the person to perform without much supervision.

Unfortunately, for some employees, job descriptions and policy statements are not specific enough to manage job behavior and performance. Likewise, simply telling the employee what is expected and what he/she is doing wrong, will never solve the problem. In our experience, it is a truism that telling people what to do is never enough.

Guiding Principle

> *For some employees, job descriptions and policy statements are not enough to manage job performance and behavior.*

Goal and Objective Setting

Think back to our lifeboat example. We said that a good leader, after assessing the general health and talent of the organization, needs to set a clear direction. This basic premise is also true for the manager. The difference is usually a question of scope. The owner sets goals for the company, whereas the manager sets goals for the unit and team. In either case, a manager can only wait so long before the team has to start rowing. Establishing goals and expectations early gives the team or the company confidence that the leader or manager knows where the company is headed.

Goals clearly define a measurable outcome or result we want to accomplish in the future. A well-written goal specifies who is responsible, the result to be achieved and a timeline.

GOAL = WHO + WHAT + WHEN

Good goals have to be attainable, but also should call for a stretch. Stretch refers to an outcome that will require an effort to attain but is still within the parameters of what is reasonably possible given the timeline. For example, in writing a sales goal, we start with the current performance; ten customer calls a week and then stretch the performance 10 to 30 percent. In this example, if our salesman, Bob, is making two calls a day (on average) or 10 a week, then we might set a goal to make three extra calls (30% increase) a week. Written out, the goal might read:

Goal: Bob in sales will increase the average number of new customer sales calls he makes from 10 to 13 calls per week by March 1, 2011.

Notice in writing a goal, we state who is responsible, the outcome or result to be achieved, the current level of performance, and the timeline for achieving the goal, all in one sentence. In setting a stretch goal, the manager is faced with the problem of small numbers and plateaus. In our experience, most performance in a title insurance company can easily improve by 10 to 30 percent, but doubling or tripling performance can be a challenge, but not in all cases. For example, years ago in a title insurance company, we visited, we discovered that one of the five examiners was examining only one file a day (on average) whereas others in the unit were doing five to nine files a day. In this instance, expecting a 100% or 200% improvement was reasonable because others were performing at that level.

On the other hand, in a unit where an escrow assistant was working on eighty files a month, expecting her to add even five more files might have been unreasonable. Typically, when the stretch required is too large, we add intermediate objectives to bridge the transition.

Objectives are a sub-set of a goal or intermediate steps or results. In theory, if the objectives are met, the goal is achieved. The difference between goals and objectives can be confusing, but the difference is actually very simple. Objectives are smaller steps of achievement toward the goal. For most large goals, there are smaller intermediate steps or objectives that can be identified. Consider the goals and objectives listed below for an escrow team. In this example, the objectives should be intermediate steps that lead to the final result. In theory, if the last objective or all the objectives are met, the goal is achieved.

Goal: The escrow processing team will work with the manager to develop a new quality checklist to use on all files by March 1, 2011.

Objectives:

1. The Processing team will meet with the manager to review and discuss past examples of checklists that have been used in other offices by 1/30.
2. The Processing team will deliver a draft checklist to the manager for review and feedback by 2-14.
3. The Processing team will provide a final draft to the Manager by 2/21.
4. The Processing team makes final changes to checklist by 3-1.

Goal: Beginning in January, the Closing Team will increase the average closings per closer per month, from 30 to 40 closing per closer per month, by September 1.

If we were to write objectives between January and September, we might divide the eight months into equal parts, for example, four month increments, and then divide the difference between the performance now (30) and the goal (40). In this way we have one goal and two objectives.

1. The Closing Team will increase the average closings per closer from 30 to 35 closings per closer per month, by May 1st.
2. The Closing Team will increase the average closings per closer from 35 to 40 closings per closer per month, by September 1st.

Guiding Principle

> **Goals clearly define a measurable outcome or result**
> **we want to accomplish in the future.**

Developing Standards

Another means for a manager to set clear expectations is by performance standards. Most of us are already familiar with the idea of performance standards. Think of a local restaurant you particularly like and frequent often. Chances are good you believe the standards for food quality and preparation, service, cleanliness of the restaurant and the restrooms, and the general appearance of the place are quite high. Now think of a restaurant that you do not like and probably went to once and swore you would never go back to again. Chances are good that you believe the overall performance of the restaurant is quite poor and significantly below the standards of the restaurant you really like.

Throughout our daily lives, we frequently apply the concept of performance standards, from the computers we use, to the cars we drive, to the shopping experience we have at a large department store, or to the shows we watch on television at night.

In the title insurance industry, performance standards help us define unacceptable, acceptable and good or outstanding levels of performance for a company, office, team as a whole, or for individual employees. Managers can on a regular basis, for example, compare the actual performance of an office with the standards that have been established.

Guiding Principle

> **Standards help us define unacceptable, acceptable and good**
> **or outstanding levels of performance.**

Visualize taking a stick and forming a straight horizontal line in the sand. The line in the sand represents the standard set for customer service. In our example, the standard set for customer service is a ranking of 4.0 using a 1 to 5 point scale, where 1 represents very poor customer service and 5 represents exceptional customer service. Performance below the line is unacceptable (scores ranging from 1 to 3.9), performance at the same level as the line (4.0) is acceptable and expected, and performance above the line is very good or exceptional customer service (scores ranging from 4.1 to 5).

Performance standards are often developed and adhered to on a company-wide basis, but managers have the opportunity to re-state the importance of established standards and to manage using them. In those cases where performance standards have not been developed, the manager has the opportunity to develop and set them.

Performance standards can be set for many types of performance, including productivity, customer service, quality; order counts, commitment turn-time, and, teamwork, among others. Performance standards need to be measurable in some way and they are often aligned with the measures an office or company uses on a regular basis. For example, a manager, after analyzing the performance and capabilities of his full service office (i.e., title and escrow combined) and talking to his staff and his supervisor, might set the following standards:

FOCUS AREA	STANDARD
• Customer Service	All customer phone calls are to be returned within one hour
• Productivity (Title Production Team as a whole)	45 title orders per person per month
• Productivity (Escrow Team as a whole)	20 closings per person per month
• Productivity (Individual Closers)	37 closings per closer per month
• Quality (Title and Escrow Teams combined)	95 percent error free files per month. 0 % critical errors.
• Team Work	Team rates, level of teamwork at 8 or higher on a 10 point rating scale

Standards are often determined by the conditions and circumstances that exist in the local market, including laws, availability of records and documents, use of technology, local customer practices, common staffing patterns and rival competition. When we work with managers in local markets we often ask about commitment turn-time. For example, a title manager in a particular market might say, "The average turn time for a residential re-sale commitment is this area is 3 days, that is the market standard. We have decided that we need to perform above that market standard. Our standard for a residential re-sale commitment is 2 days."

The local manager is referring to the average turn-time among title insurance companies in the market. He is also saying that to out-perform the competition, his company has set a higher standard (i.e., two days instead of three).

In terms of productivity, individual employee standards are often determined based on what experienced and trained employees can accomplish on average. For example, a title production manager might determine that an experienced, well-trained examiner in his office is capable of examining between eight and ten orders a day. Based on this range, the manager sets the standard at eight orders a day for all experienced examiners. Performance below eight a day is unacceptable and performance at or above eight is good to exceptional depending upon the final total.

The standards a company or office manager sets can also be driven by financial considerations. For example, a manager might say, "our standard for orders processed per month for this office is 250 orders." This means that if the office falls below 250 orders per month, the office will not meet the planned profit margin.

In other industries, the term standard can be used somewhat differently. For example, it is often said that the Ritz-Carlton hotel chain sets the standard or bar for exemplary customer service. The connotation is that if other hotels are able to match this service standard, they are performing quite well. In the title insurance industry, we never want to perform below the standards we have established. However, we do want to perform above or significantly above our standards, whenever we can.

The discussion the manager can have with his employees is to point out and discuss the standards that have been set and how close the actual performance of the office or team is to what is expected. If the actual performance is below the standards set, the manager has the opportunity to work with his team, or individual employees, to develop goals and tactics to meet and exceed the standards that have been established.

Making Goals, Objectives, and Standards Work

The development of goals and objectives and the setting of performance standards can often work in concert together. Here is an example of how goals, objectives and standards complement each other. We worked with a new manager in a title insurance company in the upstate New York region. The new manager was assuming the leadership of several offices in the area and was aware that the customer service reputation for these offices was quite low. The previous manager was also aware of the situation but was not able to make any significant improvements. We convinced the new manager to start by taking a baseline of the customer satisfaction for his offices. We helped him design and implement a customer survey that was sent to customers and the results confirmed what he and others thought to be true, the satisfaction ratings were in fact very low.

The baseline survey measurement gave us a starting point from which to plan. The results showed that the average customer satisfaction ratings were 4.0 on a 10-point rating scale where 1 equaled highly dissatisfied customers and 10 equaled highly satisfied customers. The new manager then realized the standard for satisfaction ratings for these offices needed to be set at 8.0. Indeed, the new manager also realized that he and these offices had a long way to go! The first step for us in working with the new manager was to help him develop a set of goals and objectives that would complement the standard he was setting. An example of goals and objectives, we established to support the attainment of the new standard are presented in Table7.

Communicating Expectations

As consultants, when we are asked to come into title insurance companies to discover the strengths and weaknesses of operations, employees routinely tell us the lack of communication is their number one issue. Truth be told, you can never provide too much communication to your employees. Managers must vary the types of communication they use and they must communicate frequently.

Table 7. Example of standard, goals, and objectives.

STANDARD: Average Customer Satisfaction ratings of 8.0

GOAL: The office will exceed the customer service standard by 12/1/2011

OBJECTIVES:

- Interview customers to determine customer issues by 4/1/2011.
- Form customer service team to develop a service plan by 7/1/2011.
- Pilot new service solutions and tactics by 8/1/2011.
- Implement all new service solutions and tactics in all offices by 9 /1/2011.
- Obtain an average customer satisfaction ratings of 7.0 by 9 /30/2011.
- Obtain an average customer satisfaction ratings of 8.0 or better by 12/1/2011.

Moreover, it is one thing to develop good goals and objectives and to set measurable standards, but yet another thing to communicate their use effectively. Good communication requires the manager to vary the means she uses and to communicate frequently on an ongoing basis. Performance goals, objectives and standards should not be brought out, discussed once, and then put in a drawer. Rather, they should be discussed and referred to at least monthly at staff meetings and referred to often when managers meet individually with their employees.

One of our favorite team-building activities is called "The Blindfold Order". The rules for this activity are simple. Eight members of the team are blindfolded and the remaining team members act as observers. The facilitator for the activity, then pins a number on the back of each person wearing a blindfold and whispers the number in each person's ear. The surprise is that one of the numbers is zero. The blindfolded participants are told they cannot talk in any way, nor can they make any noise using their mouths. Then, they are told as a group they must align themselves in a straight line in the correct numerical order. The team members who are observers are told to record the different types of communication they see.

What ensues is often quite amusing, but also instructive. People clap their number, they form their number in their hands and have others trace over their hands, they stomp their feet on the ground sounding out their number and they try to physically position people in a line based on what they have determined the correct order should be. The person assigned Zero, has the most difficult number to communicate. The lesson of the Blindfold Order is that communication can take on many forms, some of which we often have not considered.

Managers should continue to look for additional opportunities to direct attention to the goals and standards developed for their offices and teams. Email, newsletters, company Websites, blogs, and business networking platforms all provide opportunities for managers to direct attention to goals and standards. Formal employee performance appraisals or reviews also present a natural opportunity to discuss performance goals and standards with an employee. Managers also have the opportunity to re-focus employee attention to the vision or mission of the company, as well as company core values, and to discuss how the specific goals and standards that have been set are aligned with what employees should be doing on a daily basis.

Guiding Principle

> ***You can never communicate too much to employees.***

The following table provides several different types of communication managers should consider in general, to communicate expectations and provide consequences for performance:

MODE	EXAMPLES
• Informal	Stop and talk with someone at his or her desk, in the lunchroom, at the water cooler; or in the car on the way to a meeting with a customer.
• Electronic	Email; employee blogs on company web site; E-newsletters.
• Verbal	At staff meetings: discuss team and company performance; provide updates on company news; discuss goals and priorities.
• Written	Circulate written reports and memos; share marketing materials with employees; distribute company vision, mission, and core values.
• Body Language	Show excitement when something good in the office happens; extend a high-five; Pat someone on the back for a job well done; extend a handshake with a smile.

TAKE AWAY ACTIVITY
CHAPTER 10
SETTING EXPECTATIONS

1. Choose an employee and a performance improvement area you want to focus on. Write a stretch goal for the employee that includes a ten percent increase and clearly states who, what and when.

2. Do you have established standards in your company? What areas should you focus on for standards development?

3. What types of communication do you use in your office or with your team on a frequent basis? How have you communicated your expectations for employee performance? What additional steps could you take to improve your setting of expectations?

GUIDING PRINCIPLES
CHAPTER 10
SETTING EXPECTATIONS

1. For some employees, job descriptions and policy statements are not enough to manage job performance and behavior.

2. Goals clearly define a measurable outcome or result we want to accomplish in the future.

3. In the title insurance industry, standards help us define unacceptable, acceptable and good or outstanding levels of performance.

4. You can never provide too much communication to your employees.

SUPPORTIVE COACHING

In Chapter 11, we examine coaching individuals and teams. In sports, there are two types of coaching. There is the coaching that occurs in practice, and the coaching that occurs during the game. In practice, the coach can set up learning experiences where the player learns the right way to perform and the coach can give very specific feedback about the behavior that is expected. In training, the player can practice a behavior repeatedly until he/she gets it right. For example, in basketball a player could practice free throws, working out his / her mechanics until nearly every throw goes through the hoop.

In a game, the situation is different. Here the players are performing not practicing, and the basketball coach has a different role. During a game, the head coach often roams the sidelines calling out directions to the team. In this role, the coach yells out encouragement and praises his/her players when they perform successfully, for example "great block." Sometimes the coach is supporting the team as a whole and at other times, he or she may be directing attention or praise to individual players on the floor for their specific performance. During the game the coach is trying to motivate, encourage, and praise overall results. During the game, coaching is more about building confidence, "I know you can make this free throw," and about discipline, "do that again and you are out of the game."

In the business world, performance can be practiced and planned, but often coaching is spontaneous and must happen on the job. When a manager sees an employee behaving in a certain way and he/she wants to reward or praise that behavior, the manager can spontaneously go up to the employee and say something like, "I like the fact that you are using our quality check list on each file. Keep up the good work."

Whether feedback is spontaneous or carefully planned, there are several tactics a manager in the title insurance industry should consider to improve their supportive coaching. In this chapter, we will examine two types of feedback, positive feedback and constructive feedback and then discuss several tactics managers can use to sharpen their overall supportive coaching approach.

Providing Feedback

When we interview employees, the number one complaint about any business owner or manager is he/she does not communicate enough. Perhaps the second most common statement or desire is for an evaluation of the work. Employees will say, "I want to know how I am doing." Fundamental to being an effective manager is providing employees with timely and unbiased evaluations of the employees' behavior and performance. For the supportive coach, providing honest, unbiased, objective observations related to the employees work is critical. Providing performance feedback is also critical. Employees want feedback, but feedback about performance and general behavior can have negative consequences, and the wise manager should be clear on what tactics will work best in certain situations.

Guiding Principle

> ### *Employees want feedback on how they are doing.*

Feedback can take many forms. Every day there are opportunities for feedback. There are two main types of feedback: (1) positive feedback and (2) constructive feedback. We use positive feedback when we want to encourage and reward behavior that is appropriate, outstanding, or for behavior that is being trained. We use constructive feedback when we want to focus on behavior that needs to be improved or changed in some fashion. Both types of feedback are used by managers depending upon the situation and the specific employee or team involved. Many people believe that you should not mix the two at the same time because you may send conflicting messages to the employee or team. It is our opinion that effective coaches are able to differentiate what was praise worthy and what needs to improve, but if you are starting out, we recommend starting with positive (praise) feedback, and then in a separate setting, offering constructive feedback. One of the oldest techniques used by coaches and managers is the idea of sandwiching bad news (constructive feedback) between statements of praise. "I like this, I like this, this could improve, I like this, and this is great."

Positive Feedback

Positive feedback is a way of encouraging specific behaviors, performance, or outcomes. It includes verbal acknowledgment of expected work done well. Positive feedback is a tactic managers use to provide positive consequences. For example:

- "Thanks for getting that file to me on time, I checked it over and the documents and numbers all look good."

It can occur in written form, for example, when you send an email:

- "Thanks Jim for staying late yesterday and finishing the work on those two late new orders that came in. We have been waiting to get orders from those two new customers and I think your quick response will make a great first impression."

Feedback can also include a physical component such as a friendly pat on the back or a high five when something has been accomplished and you want to put an exclamation point on the verbal feedback you have provided. Feedback can be informal, when a manager walks through the office and observes something positive, she has the opportunity to praise or comment (provide feedback) on what she observed. Feedback can be formal, for example, when a manager asks an employee to participate in a private one-on-one meeting to review the employee's performance. When you provide positive feedback, remember these five simple rules:

1. Pinpoint the behavior. Specify the behavior in question.
2. Make sure the employee has direct control over the behavior you are pinpointing.
3. Be timely, the closer feedback is to when the behavior occurred, the better.
4. Identify examples of situations where the behavior occurred.
5. Add an evaluative expression, for example "that was good."

For written feedback it is important to be concise. If the written message is too long, the employee will not read it. For written feedback, include measurement when possible. For example, include a number, a table, or a chart of some type. Finally, if you provide written feedback, date the document and keep a copy.

Timeliness is important in providing good feedback and when possible, immediate feedback is best, especially when an employee has done something new that you want to encourage. We once worked with a Sales Manager who was trying to get his Account Managers to be more specific when filling out their daily call reports. His sales people had already complained that they had too much paper work to do so this new request from the Manager was not going to be easy. The Manager provided several good antecedents for the new behavior, he was expecting: He met with the Account Managers and discussed the importance of better call reports and provided a rationale; He explained how more specific information would help the company better target customer needs; He provided specific examples of what he was expecting; He then sent reminder emails to the Account Managers at the beginning of each week.

For the first two weeks the call reports from most of the Account Managers were significantly better. Unfortunately, the Manager decided to provide feedback on the improvement during his quarterly sales meeting, which was two months away. By the end of the first month the sales staff had slipped back to providing only minimal information in their call reports. In coaching sessions with the Manager we explained the importance of timely feedback and praise and recommended the Manager start providing daily feedback to the Account Reps for one week followed by once a week feedback until the next sales meeting. The improvements were significant and by the time of the next sales meeting the Manager was able to tell the sales staff that 95% of the call reports were meeting the new criteria and the improved information had already been linked to several new orders.

In general, the longer the period between when employee behavior occurs and positive feedback occurs, the less effective it will be. Daily feedback is very good, but not always possible, weekly feedback is effective in many types of situations, but monthly feedback or longer will not be as effective. In working with employees on developing new skills and behaviors, timely and frequent feedback will be the best procedure to use.

Pointing out examples of behavior pinpoints is a good way to add further specificity to your feedback. For example, when an escrow manager decided to provide feedback to her receptionist about a behavior pinpoint they had discussed, she decided to refer to an observation she had made the day before. The behavior pinpoint was saying, "Hello, how may I help you," when customers entered the office. The escrow manager provided this feedback:

> *Jackie, I noticed yesterday that when you greeted the customer by saying 'hello, how may I help you', you raised the inflection of your voice and your smile was terrific. That was excellent, keep up the good work!*

In her feedback, the manager referred to the pinpoint, pointed out a specific example, she had observed, elaborated, and added an evaluative phrase. Providing examples adds greater clarity to your feedback and employees easily relate to behavior they have performed.

When we provide feedback for employee behavior we need to make certain that the employee has direct control over the behavior or outcome we are commenting on or praising. For example, let us say we are working with an office receptionist and we want to provide feedback on her actual performance. For example, the receptionist answer phones, greets customers as they enter the office, sorts office mail and signs off on packages and deliveries received, and escorts customers to the closing rooms. These are all specific behaviors over which she has direct control. These are the specific behaviors that we should provide feedback on and praise. If we want to praise the receptionist for improving customer service in the office, we would want to point out specific behaviors that she had control over. For example, answering the phone within a specified period; saying, "Hello, how may I help you?" when customers entered into the reception area; and entering all new orders received from walk-ins within one hour. Remember how we said the level of praise should match the behavior in question? The same is true for the outcome being recognized, it has to match what the employee has control over. For example, we could thank the receptionist for the increase in market share this month because of her great customer service, but she would likely think the feedback was insincere and at best meaningless because the connection between her daily behavior and increased market share is far removed.

Guiding Principle

> **We use positive feedback to encourage and reward appropriate behavior and results.**

What opportunities do you have to provide positive feedback throughout the day? Identify an employee you manage and list four examples of positive feedback you can provide. In your list, pinpoint the behavior you are providing feedback for, make sure the employee has direct control over the behavior, and identify how and when you will provide the feedback.

Constructive Feedback

Constructive Feedback is a way to pinpoint behavior that we want to stop or lessen and encourage behavior or results we want to increase. When managers provide constructive feedback they want to do it in a way that is supportive but at the same time direct and clear. The following are guidelines to consider when providing constructive feedback:

1. Pinpoint the results or behavior that needs to change or improve.
2. Explain the reason why the specific behavior needs to change.
3. Provide examples if possible.
4. Be clear on what you expect in the future.
5. Offer assistance in terms of supporting the employee.
6. Ask the employee for input.

When providing constructive feedback we start by pinpointing the specific results or behavior that needs to change or improve. In the title insurance industry we might provide constructive feedback to employees for the following problem behaviors:

- Coming to work late.
- Making promises to customers regarding commitment turn time without checking first with the title department.
- Talking negatively about the company in front of team members.
- Complaining about customers.
- Complaining about co-workers.
- Dressing inappropriately.
- Quitting work early (not working during the last 30 minutes).
- Meeting the standard for number of commitments produced.

- Meeting the standard for number of closings in a month.
- Providing status updates to the customer for new orders received.
- Using the company's quality checklist when processing files.
- Checking HUD numbers twice before proceeding.
- Volunteering to conduct remote or late closings.

When providing constructive feedback it is important to explain to the employee why the behavior in question has to change or improve. Here is an example of a manager providing constructive feedback to an employee about the importance of customer service.

Jamie, I have noticed that you are not returning customer phone calls in a timely fashion. I checked the phone log this week and there were five calls for you that were received early in the morning and were not returned until late in the afternoon. As you know, our standard for returning customer phone calls is to respond to the customer within one hour. Remember, one of our core values is providing superior customer service. Returning customer phone calls within one hour is an example of how we provide superior customer service. I need you to start meeting our standard for returning phone calls, on a daily basis. If you are going to have a problem in returning a call within one hour I want you to notify your immediate supervisor and arrange for someone else to take care of the call. Do you have any additional ideas that would help us help you?

Note that in the above example the manager pinpointed the behavior that needs to improve (returning phone calls in less than one hour). The manager explained the reason for why returning calls in a timely fashion are important (it is a core value providing superior customer service). The manager provided examples and evidence of the problem (there were five calls this week that did not meet the standard) and was clear to what is expected in the future (Jamie to start meeting the company's standard on a daily basis). Finally, the manager offered assistance and asked Jamie for input (the manager instructed Jamie to let his supervisor know if there was a problem in returning a call and asked Jamie if he had any additional ideas).

Providing constructive feedback is an important procedure you can use to correct a pattern of behavior in an employee that needs to be changed or improved. Key to the use of constructive feedback is following up with the use of positive feedback or positive consequences as soon as possible to strengthen the behavior you are trying to develop.

Guiding Principle

> *We use constructive feedback to focus on behavior and results that needs to be improved or changed.*

In the case of Jamie, the manager needs to be looking for the next time Jamie returns a call within the specified time. When that happens the manager needs to provide positive feedback, praise and reward the timely behavior and continue to find ways to reward the correct behavior in the days and weeks that follow. In addition to paying attention to employee behavior, managers, in their role as supportive coaches, must also keep in mind their own behavior.

Guiding Principle

> *Positive feedback is a tactic managers use to provide positive consequences.*

The Eight Bs

The Eight Bs is a list of behaviors that every supportive coach must be aware of and be prepared to be.

1. **Be a good listener and observer.** Conduct a daily "walk around" the office to catch specific behaviors to reward. Remember the idea of "Catch 'em being good."
2. **Be timely.** Timeliness is a key in providing positive feedback and consequences to employees. In the beginning when trying to increase specific behavior, deliver positive consequences soon after the behavior occurs. Too far past the target behavior in question will be ineffective. As you start to see progress, you can vary the intervals and timing of your use of positive feedback and consequences.
3. **Be consistent:** Do not announce or discuss a promise or incentive and not follow-through. If you tell an employee, you will give them feedback, then provide it in a timely fashion. If you say to your team you will buy coffee and doughnuts for the group if they meet their weekly performance goal, you have to deliver if they meet their goal.
4. **Be unpredictable.** Once you have provided timely feedback and positive consequences, start varying the time intervals you use and the types of positive feedback and rewards. Use a number of rewards and consequences, and vary your consequences, for example, leave a note, deliver praise in private, praise in front of others, give a financial reward. Remember, variety is important and will keep the employee interested.
5. **Be encouraging.** Break your goal into smaller steps, provide feedback, and reward progress along the way.
6. **Be patient.** Change and improvement are not simple, they take a while. There will be back steps and small failures. Be patient and keep at it.
7. **Be accessible.** As a supportive coach, your presence and availability will be key to some employees.
8. **Be specific.** When providing feedback and praising an employee, be specific and pinpoint:
   a. "I liked how you volunteered for cleanup."
   b. You sounded very pleasant on the phone just now. I like your overall tone and inflection"
   c. "The fact that you stayed late to finish the file for the customer was excellent."

Self-Evaluation: Supportive Coach

Below is a self-evaluation checklist you can use to monitor whether you are being a good supportive coach. Notice that in the checklist we have provided general supportive concepts or ideas that managers should emulate and example corresponding behavior pinpoints. Review the general supporting concept first and then examine the examples of specific behavior managers can emulate. As you go through our list, check off the tactics you need to improve on.

1. **I set clear expectations.** I meet with employees and discuss what I expect from them. I pinpoint behavior with timelines; I discuss ways performance will be measured and evaluated.

2. **I provide praise often.** For example, I do a morning walk around the office and seek out employees to praise. I acknowledge employees at weekly staff meetings. I send thank you notes to employees via emails.

3. **I encourage my employees.** I refer to the company core values often in team meetings; I discuss team goals often and work with my team to set new goals. I sit down with individual employees often and find positive things to say about their work.

4. **I provide feedback often.** I review weekly performance and discuss results with my team and with individual employees. I provide constructive feedback pointing out what behavior needs to improve and why. When an employee is learning a new skill or procedure, I increase my frequency of feedback.

5. **I am positive and enthusiastic.** I pump my fists in public and clap a lot when we meet our goals. I like to start the morning by announcing, "It's a great day for title insurance!" Each day I try to find something to comment on that is positive.

6. **I am accessible daily.** I circulate my schedule each week so employees know where I will be. When I am in the office, I have a standard two-hour period my door is always open. I spend the first 30 minutes of each day walking around the office and meeting and talking with staff.

7. **I am a good listener.** I try not to talk first when an employee comes to me with a question. I look directly at the employee and maintain eye contact. I repeat back to the employee what I have understood they said.

8. **I focus on specific behavior the employee is doing.** I pinpoint behavior when I praise. I pinpoint behavior when I provide feedback. I pinpoint behavior when I provide constructive feedback.

9. **I am observant of employee behavior on a daily basis.** I go into the reception area and observe how employees greet customers. I sit in on closings to observe how different documents are described. I go on sales calls with Account Reps to observe the needs assessment questions we ask customers.

10. **I am goal oriented when I coach.** I explain how specific behavior pinpoints will lead to the results we want. I review team goals with my team. I review individual goals with employees.

11. **I vary my types of consequences.** I determine which types of praise will work the best with specific employees. My ratio of positive consequences to constructive feedback is about 4:1. I use social and tangible consequences and look to arrange activities so that the completion of certain tasks leads to the opportunity to work on more appealing tasks.

12. **My employees respect and trust me.** I follow through on things I promise or say I will do. I involve employees in decision-making and ask for their input. I roll up my sleeves and work alongside employees when it is needed.

13. **I hold effective team meetings.** I plan and circulate agenda ahead of each meeting. I keep meetings to set time parameters and start and end on time. I use meetings to provide positive feedback to my team. I vary topics to keep interest up and circulate meeting summaries to staff.

14. **I review employee performance on a weekly basis.** I review performance reports. I review individual employee goals and team goals. I compare employee and team performance to company-wide performance results.

15. **I ask for feedback from my employees.** In team meetings, I ask for employee input. I encourage individual employees to come to me with ideas. I ask employees to tell me what resources they need and how I can manage them better.

Sometimes a behavior problem continues, even in the presence of supportive coaching and feedback. In the next chapter, we will examine what managers can do when behavior and performance problems persist.

TAKE AWAY ACTIVITY
CHAPTER 11
SUPPORTIVE COACHING

1. Consider the Eight Bs. What "Be" do you need to work on most. Pick an employee or a situation where you can engage in that "B," and try it.

2. Complete the self-assessment and evaluate your level of management coaching. What are you already doing? What could you improve?

GUIDING PRINCIPLES
CHAPTER 11
SUPPORTIVE COACHING

1. Employees want feedback on how they are doing.

2. We use positive feedback to encourage and reward appropriate behavior and results.

3. We use constructive feedback to focus on behavior and results that needs to be improved or changed.

4. Positive feedback is a tactic managers use to provide positive consequences.

MANAGING PROBLEMS

So far, we have used supportive coaching to encourage desired behavior and to correct an existing problem. Sometimes a behavior or performance problem persists even in the presence of supportive and constructive coaching. For example, when a manager has encouraged and praised an employee when he is on time and provided constructive feedback when he is late. In the face of timely feedback, attention and constructive feedback, you would think the employee's behavior would change, but sometimes it does not.

In Chapter 12, we discuss how managers can proceed in a systematic way when behavior and performance problems persist. In doing so, we focus on how to prepare for and conduct a formal sit down meeting with an employee. Often times, when a problem persists, we first recommend taking a step back and further analyzing the situation. Here are the steps we follow when dealing with a performance or a behavior problem that has persisted for an extended period.

1. Pinpoint the specific problem behavior, i.e., the behavior that needs to change or improve. This is the present or current state.

2. Pinpoint the desired behavior or the outcome that needs to be achieved. This is the future state, what we want to occur.

3. Analyze the situation (antecedents and consequences) surrounding each behavior or outcome defined in Steps One and Two. We analyze if there are any factors that may be contributing to the employee's current behavior or if there are supportive factors that are missing.

Consider the example of an employee who complains about co-workers to other employees. Our first two steps are to pinpoint the current problem behavior and then pinpoint what behavior we want in the future. What is important in this process is understanding that the desired outcome is not always the mirror opposite of the problem.

Guiding Principle

> **Pinpoint the desired behavior**

In our example, the problem behavior is complaining about co-workers to other employees. Is the desired behavior, saying positive things about co-workers to other employees or is the desired behavior not complaining? Pinpointing the present behavior you want to stop or lessen and the future behavior you desire are the first steps in any problem solving.

Guiding Principle

> **Pinpoint the problem behavior**

In our third step, we analyze the conditions that exist surrounding the current problem behavior. To aid in our analysis, we ask a number of questions we refer to as a Situational Analysis.

Situational Analysis Questions

1. What is the current problem behavior?
2. What is the desired (expected) future behavior?
3. Have the expected behaviors been communicated to the employee?
4. Does the employee know what behavior or outcome is expected?
5. Does the employee want to perform the behavior or believe the behavior or outcome is important?
6. Has the employee ever performed the behavior or produced the outcome desired?
   a. If yes, the behavior has occurred in the past, is it now absent?
   b. If yes, the behavior has occurred in the past, is it now inconsistent?
   c. If no, are there obstacles or other priorities that are preventing the employee from behaving?

7. What are the consequences for behaving in the ways that are expected?
8. What are the consequences for not doing what is desired or for engaging in the problem behavior?
9. What is the employee's input or solution to the problem?

Answering any of these situational questions may require talking to the employee, observing the situation, and talking to others. Consider the example of Bill the Examiner. In Bill's company the standard for title examination is an average of eight residential re-sale commitments a day. The problem is Bill is not examining eight title commitments per day and he is not averaging eight a day. He had four days out of twenty in the last month where he examined eight files, but the other fifteen days averaged less than six a day. In trying to solve this problem, we follow the situational analysis steps. After pinpointing the current performance problem and the performance we want in the future, the next question is whether the company standard (expectation) has been made explicitly clear to Bill. For example, the standard could have been discussed at the point of hire, it could have been discussed at monthly staff meetings, or it could have been made clear to the employee during a yearly performance review. As surprising as it sounds, performance expectations are not often made clear to employees. Therefore the employee has no basis for judging his/her performance. If performance expectations have not been made clear, it is often a simple starting point. Tell the employee what you expect. Sometimes simply making expectations clear is the correct antecedent to get the behavior started in the right direction.

The next question in a situational analysis is whether the employee wants to perform the behavior or believes it is important. If the employee does not believe there is a problem; if the employee does not accept his/her behavior is a problem; if the employee does not accept and take responsibility for changing his/her behavior, nothing will happen.

Guiding Principle

> ### The employee must agree that a problem exists

Meeting with the Employee

To answer whether an employee accepts responsibility for changing, to further analyze antecedents and consequences, and gain employee input, you may need to conduct a formal meeting with the employee. In our example, Bill told his manager, he did not think producing eight title exams per day was possible, let alone important. Bill argued that all exams were different, you had to allow for those differences and some exams would just take longer. The manager reminded Bill there were two other examiners on staff who had the same level of experience, he did who were performing consistently above the standard of eight exams per day. The manager also showed a performance report to Bill that tracked his weekly and monthly performance. The report clearly showed there were several times in the past Bill had either met or exceeded the daily standard of eight exams per day. Bill acted surprised when he saw the report and said he was not aware he had produced that many title commitments. In fact, upon closer examination, Bill saw there was typically at least one day each week when he did meet the productivity standard.

The manager then asked Bill if there were any obstacles or other priorities preventing him from meeting the daily productivity standard. Bill indicated he was pulled away from his work quite frequently during the day to answer questions about problems of a curative nature with other files and he thought that often got him off track. Bill indicated he found curative work interesting and liked doing it. He also said he did have issues in terms of how to prioritize which orders to work on each day.

In reflecting on his own behavior, the manager realized he had not provided enough feedback to Bill on a weekly basis. He knew he had often reminded Bill he needed to produce more, but realized he had not provided consistent feedback and praise on those days when Bill did produce the number of commitments needed. The manager then asked Bill what he thought might help solve the problem in the future. Bill indicated that reviewing daily his commitment total would be helpful and seeing a report at the end of a week would help him keep on track. He said he would also like to talk to the other examiners to learn how they prioritized their daily work. The manager also agreed there were steps in the workflow that could be changed that would limit the amount of curative work Bill would need to do on a daily basis. The manager said he realized now that Bill liked to do the curative work but a higher priority for the company was for him to meet the daily productivity standard. The Manager and Bill agreed to which corrective steps they both would take in the coming weeks and agreed on a date to meet again to review progress on the plan they had developed.

Talking with the employee in a formal meeting requires preparation. It is important that you plan ahead to meet with the employee. In this meeting, you want to clearly specify what needs to change and how.

Guiding Principle

> **A formal meeting with an employee requires preparation.**

In your first meeting, consider using the following structure:

1. Explain the purpose of the meeting.
2. Discuss the employee's recent performance, be specific and use facts and measures.
3. Pinpoint the specific behavior or performance that needs to improve or change.
4. Pinpoint the result or behavior that needs to be achieved. Turn a negative into a positive. Specify what is to occur rather than what is not to occur.
5. Make sure the employee understands what behavior or outcome needs to occur. Have the person describe the outcome or behavior that is needed.
6. Make sure the employee agrees that improvement is necessary.
7. Mutually discuss a plan to achieve what is expected. Make sure the employee's ideas and input are part of the plan. Discuss antecedents and consequences that are missing and needed.
8. Mutually discuss any support the employee needs.
9. Commit to an action plan with timelines and responsibilities.
10. Set a date for a follow-up meeting with the employee to review performance and amend the action plan if necessary.
11. Provide the employee with a written copy of his/her plan.
12. Follow up informally before the next meeting.

In your meeting, it will be important to speak clearly, be direct and to the point. This meeting is part of your formal management or discipline of the employee. In talking with the employee, be specific and never use phrases that suggest the meeting is informal, secret, or "just between you and me."

Having a set of organized facts, dates, or data regarding the employee's current performance, if available, can make all the difference in this type of problem solving meeting. Under no conditions does the manager want this type of meeting to turn into a he said/ she said or even worse, I say / you say confrontation. In the end, what is critical is that the employee agrees with what is being discussed and accepts responsibility.

During this meeting it is critical that you make sure you obtain agreement from the employee that the specific behavior change or performance improvement is necessary. Think of this like any other human problem where self-control or personal change is part of the solution, for example quitting smoking, exercising more, or weight loss. Until the person accepts personal responsibility, no plan of action, short of firing the employee will work. Until the employee agrees and commits to change, you should not go any further. If you have a case where you do not believe the employee accepts his/her responsibility, end the meeting early, send the employee home for a day or two and ask him/her to only return when he/she is ready to accept responsibility.

Employee ownership and investment in the action plan is also crucial. The more you are able to gain and use employee ideas and input, the better. Employees will often work harder to improve if they know it is their ideas that are being used as a part of the change process. They also will work harder when they know their behavior or performance is being measured.

Remember our management truism "if you measure it, they do it." As part of any problem solving, you need to measure the behavior that needs to improve and then provide feedback. Many behavior or performance outcomes, by their very nature, are easy to measure, because they leave a record; they either happen or they do not. For example, take the behavior pinpoint: "Turns in sales report each Friday." If the measure is "turning in sales reports," the report is either present or it is not. Measuring behavior or performance can be as simple as checking off a list, tallying, or counting the behavior when it occurs. The more complicated the measure, the more indirect the measure, or the more distant in time the measure, the less effective the measure and feedback will be. Remember the example of the Sales Manager who waited for two months to provide feedback on call reports, providing feedback in the beginning daily and then at weekly intervals proved to be much more effective.

When possible, we like to take a baseline measurement to determine the current level of performance before the plan is put into effect. Taking a baseline is not always possible due to the urgency of the situation, but when it is possible, we recommend it.

For example, we worked with a manager who had an employee who was very rude and often obstinate with her fellow teammates. She also openly said negative thinks about the company in front of her team during the day. The manager had provided constructive feedback to the worker on several occasions, but the inappropriate behavior had continued. The manager decided she could not wait any longer and we helped her plan a formal sit down meeting with the employee. Luckily the manager had kept a record of the frequency and dates when team members had complained and when she personally had observed the employee's rude or inappropriate behavior. The managers four weeks of record keeping provided important baseline data she was able to use in her formal sit down meeting with the employee. If you are planning a formal sit down meeting with an employee for a problem behavior, consider these final points:

Do not over manage the exception. Often times when we talk to a manager about a problem or issue they have noticed or observed, the first question we ask is "Is what you are describing the exception or does the behavior occur frequently and consistently?" We encourage managers to use constructive feedback when they start to observe possible problem behaviors, but employee behavior that is the exception to the rule, with normally productive and excellent employees, should not be over managed. Formal sit down meetings with employees about problems should be held after coaching and constructive feedback has not resulted in necessary improvements and when inappropriate behavior continues to occur frequently and consistently.

The manager is an important part of the solution. If we did not have employees with problems, we would not need managers. This statement is of course an over simplification, but the point is the manager must play an important role in helping to solve the issue or problem at hand. Managers must first work to understand and analyze what is occurring in the problem situation and then work with the employee as a resource to solve it.

Guiding Principle

> **Managers must determine what support
> they can provide to be a part of the solution.**

Do not make measurement an afterthought. Many employees will want to challenge the fact they are behaving inappropriately. If you have measurement data to back up your behavior pinpoints, you will be in a strong position.

Guiding Principle

> **Measurement is a key in managing performance and
> behavior problems.**

Check with your HR department. Before you plan a formal sit down meeting with an employee to discuss a problem behavior or issue, make sure you are in compliance with your company HR procedures.

TAKE AWAY ACTIVITY
CHAPTER 12
MANAGING PROBLEMS

1. Pinpoint several examples of behavior or performance problems you have experienced with employees in the past.

2. For each of your behavior or performance pinpoints, did you have adequate measurement data to use? If not, what measures could you have used or put in place?

3. Choose one of your examples and complete a situational analysis of the behavior or performance problem. Refer to our nine situational analysis questions to help with your analysis.

4. What should you do on a proactive basis next time when you are faced with a persistent behavior or performance problem?

GUIDING PRINCIPLES
CHAPTER 12
MANAGING PROBLEMS

1. Pinpoint the employee's current behavior and the behavior you need to see in the future.

2. The employee must agree that a problem exists before you can proceed.

3. A formal meeting with an employee requires preparation.

4. Managers must determine what they can provide to be a part of the solution.

5. Measurement is a key in managing performance and behavior problems.

WHY MEETINGS ARE IMPORTANT

In Chapter 13, we examine the components of an effective meeting, for example, starting on time, following rules, having snacks, and using icebreakers. We also consider two essential meeting tools, brainstorming and problem solving. Finally, we recommend developing templates for frequent meetings so that new managers do not have to reinvent the wheel.

Someone once said that meetings are like going to the dentist. You know they are probably a good idea, at least in theory, but in practice, meetings are something we avoid, delay, or cancel. The fact is that most people generally hate going to meetings because the meetings they have attended were a waste of time, boring, and poorly conducted. In this judgment, we could not agree more. However, we also know that meetings do not have to be that way. A meeting can be fun, very worthwhile, stimulating, informative, result in important ideas and decisions and meetings can be an important use of your time as a leader and manager. In fact, conducting effective meetings on a regular basis should be a part of a manager's basic skill set.

Guiding Principle

> **Conducting an effective meeting should be a part of every manager's basic skill set.**

Preparation

Conducting an effective meeting requires preparation ahead of the meeting. In preparing, the manager starts by writing out the objectives for the meeting. Meetings that are held for a special reason or will be a one-time occurrence are easier to plan for because often the purpose is more narrowly focused. The objectives of a meeting should not be confused with the agenda, however, in regularly scheduled meetings; the agenda can take on the appearance of the objectives. Objectives are outcomes. Agenda items are actions. For example, the purpose of a special meeting could be to select a restaurant for the Christmas dinner. The agenda item might be to discuss locations for the Christmas dinner. If the group talks about various restaurants without selecting a place to eat, they will have completed the agenda item, but failed to meet the purpose of the meeting. When this happens, the meeting is a failure.

Routine meetings, the ones that are scheduled on a regular basis, for example every Monday or the first Monday of each month, are the easiest to set objectives and prepare an agenda for and yet, they are the hardest to get right. Often, part of the failure is keeping the meeting interesting and a failure to accomplish the meetings objectives. Regardless of the type of meeting being planned, the manager should identify realistic, tangible, and measurable outcomes for the meeting along with an agenda. The agenda and expected outcomes should be communicated ahead of time.

People attending the meeting should know ahead of time the meeting agenda and purpose. We recommend sending out the agenda two or three days before the scheduled meeting date. To gain added investment in interest and participation, ask participants to suggest additional agenda items as you distribute the agenda ahead of time. In addition to communicating the purpose and agenda, sometimes a manager will want the group to prepare information for the meeting or come prepared for some specific action or discussion. Whether you are planning to solve a problem, brainstorm new ideas, convey information, gain input from your employees, or make a decision, the more information provided ahead of the meeting, the more likely the attendees will come prepared and participate. In general, we dislike FYI meetings because the employees' only role is listening. Regardless of the purpose of the meeting or the size of the audience, we recommend that every person be assigned a role or have a task they complete and bring to the meeting.

In many of the title insurance agencies where we have worked, we have developed a standard set of meetings (e.g., weekly, monthly, and quarterly) for the owners and managers. For some meetings, we have established a template. The advantage of the template is that managers can use the templates written agenda and objectives as a starting point for planning their own meeting.

Table 8. Example of an executive meeting template

Monthly Manager Meeting
Attendees: Owners, President, Vice Presidents, Managers.
Agenda:
1. Review the agenda for the meeting.
   - o Have copies in front of each participant.
   - o Display agenda on a screen using a computer projector, monitor, or write the agenda on a flip chart.
   - o Point out the items that were added by the meeting participants.
   - o Point out items from prior meetings.
2. Present and discuss performance results on key measures.
   - o Discuss results for the month compared to the prior month and the same month last year. For example, new orders, closings, average turn-time, average income per order, closings per full-time equivalent (FTE), and evidence of customer satisfaction.
   - o Discuss year to date results (YTD) comparisons to the prior year, and any trends for key measures.
3. Present and discuss company news and information.
   - o Review new management decisions or directives.
   - o Review new company initiatives.
   - o Review HR issues.
   - o Review any new policies or procedures.
   - o Facilitate a Q & A on company issues.
   - o Open the floor to a discussion of employee issues and needs. Ask for staff input on office progress and issues that needs to be addressed.
4. Highlight local, state, regional or national news affecting the title business.
5. Summarize meeting results.
   - o Review what agenda items were completed
   - o Review any items placed on hold
   - o Review any decisions made along with timelines, responsible parties, and any specific actions.
   - o Send out a one-page summary of the meeting results to the meeting participants.

Optional Agenda Items:
- Identify new customers.
  - o Discuss new customers and the special tactics needed to ensure good new customer impressions.
- Discuss employee highlights / issues.
  - o Single out significant employee achievements or highlight excellent customer service stories, emphasizing employee involvement.
- Provide an educational component.
  - o Discuss a new idea or trend in the title insurance industry that is of interest and that may in the future impact operations in some way.
- Invite a guest speaker.
  - o Bring someone from another department or unit of the company.
  - o Invite a professional from an affiliated company.
  - o Invite a specialist from an underwriter.
  - o Invite a customer to come and discuss their business and their business needs.

Arrive Prepared. This sounds like a simple idea, but the number of managers who make the mistake of walking into a meeting unprepared and try to wing it would surprise you. Employees always know when a manager is not prepared. Spend time ahead of the meeting to go over each agenda item. Say the agenda aloud. Know the main discussion points you will be bringing before your group. If you will have handouts to distribute make sure they are organized and ready to go. If you are using media equipment during the meeting, make sure it is on site and tested before the meeting begins. Consider your time management and how much time you should spend on each agenda item. If you have put more items on the agenda than time will permit for good discussion, better to scale back the agenda ahead of time rather than trying to do too much in not enough time. It is better to cover five agenda items well versus ten agenda items poorly in the same amount of time. If you will be asking other participants to present ideas or lead a portion of the discussion, check with them ahead of time to make sure they are prepared.

Conducting the Meeting

Start on Time. Starting your meeting on time is one of the most important things you can do. It sends the simple message that you respect those team members who have arrived on time and that you are professional and efficient. It also provides an excellent model for other managers on how they should conduct their own meetings. Start by reviewing your agenda, make any necessary additions or adjustments, and thank participants for their time. Review the meeting ground rules if necessary, especially if you are starting with a new team. Consider identifying a person to record minutes for the meeting. The recorder will capture the major decisions and actions taken at the meeting and then distribute them to the meeting participants. Most meetings do not need formal minutes to be taken; we prefer a simple written summary that highlights what was decided, responsibilities and timelines. The agenda can be attached to the one page summary, if necessary so that everyone can look back on the entire scope of what was discussed. Meeting summaries are important because they foster good communication, keep everyone on the same page, and are a good tool to use in following up on timelines and responsibilities. Before any notes are communicated to the team or general workforce, make sure the notes to be communicated are reviewed for spelling and grammar, accuracy, and content. We often suggest that managers use them at the start of each new meeting as a quick follow-up review.

Guiding Principle

> **Good meetings require preparation.**

Icebreakers. A great way to energize a meeting is to start with an icebreaker. We have witnessed many people roll their eyes and appear skeptical when we have first announced the idea to start a meeting with an ice-breaker, only to find just a few minutes later the entire group laughing, interacting and generally acting enthused. Using the web is a good source for finding icebreakers. We have used several good icebreakers from a book by West[7].

Guiding Principle

> **Icebreakers energize meetings and make them fun.**

Here is an icebreaker that is a favorite of ours for a group meeting together for the first time. It is easy to use and will get everyone talking and participating:

The Name Game:

1. Ahead of your meeting, purchase tent cards and markers for each person. You can also simply have participants do this with a piece of paper folded lengthwise in three. If the participants will not be sitting at a table, use stick-on name badges.
2. At the meeting, have the participant print his/her first name on the right half of the tent card. Make sure you show an example before anyone gets a pen.
3. Announce that for the meeting, everyone will have a new name. Ask each participant to develop a new name that utilizes the same first letter of their first name and is descriptive of the person's personality. They are to write their new names on the left half of the tent placards. Again, show an example. For

---

[7] Edie West . The Big Book of Icebreakers: Quick, Fun Activities for Energizing Meetings and Workshops. New York, McGraw-Hill, 1999.

example, "Chris" might be paired with "Charismatic Chris," and Roger might be paired with "Rowdy Roger."

4. Give the group a few minutes to develop their names, write them down and position their placards in front of them. Then go around the group individually asking each group member to announce his/her new name. Comment on each name selection or ask other group members to respond in kind.

5. Require that the group use the new names for the remainder of the meeting. Anticipate quite a bit of laughing and good cheer about the name selections and a great start to your meeting!

Establishing Meeting Ground Rules. Good meetings have ground rules. These should not be complicated, but they should convey not only the general parameters for how the meeting will be conducted, but also specify what responsibilities participants have during the meeting. We like to develop our meeting ground rules ahead of time and bring them to discuss and distribute at the beginning of the first meeting. You can add them to your agenda or bring them as a separate handout. Another option is to have them available for everyone to see on a flip chart or screen. If you are meeting with a new team, a good activity is to ask the group to develop the ground rules with you. Below is a short list of ground rules we have used.

1. Everyone speaks.
2. Do not hold back your feelings be direct and honest.
3. Ask questions.
4. Agree to disagree.
5. Listen to each other.
6. Be constructively critical.
7. Be open to the ideas of others.
8. Stay on task and be focused.
9. Recognize team members and be supportive.
10. Promote good teamwork.

Guiding Principle

Use a meeting recorder (note taker) to capture important actions and decisions.

Stick to the Agenda. If you are conducting the meeting, it is critical to stick to the agenda and yet allow adequate time for each agenda item. When you facilitate a meeting, your role is to keep the discussion moving. If you observe that there are team members who are not participating, your role is to get them involved in the discussion. Do not hesitate to be direct and ask team members for their opinions and ideas. You will not be doing your team justice if only a few members are actively participating.

Do not wait to evaluate your meeting until after the meeting is over. Be aware of how your team is interacting, their level of attention and enthusiasm as the meeting progresses. We call this being under the control of our audience. If you see several team members who are yawning or closing their eyes, you need to make some adjustments.

The Bucket Rule. In our experience, one of the things that destroy a meeting is an argument that goes beyond constructive criticism and good debate. The bucket is a procedure we use to stop that type of argument. The bucket rule is simple, the meeting facilitator, or anyone in the group, can say "bucket" and the topic under discussion can be shelved until the end of the meeting or until the next meeting. Under the bucket rule, nothing more may be said. The facilitator can assume the ultimate responsibility of determining if an agenda item should be "bucketed".

Guiding Principle

Use the Bucket rule to table an item whose discussion becomes unconstructive or is taking up too much of the agenda time.

As a facilitator, conflict of any kind needs to be avoided, and yet, when a group is discussing a difficult issue, it is likely some participants will have strong opinions. When you are facilitating a discussion, constructive criticism can be important, but any disagreement must not turn into a he-said-she-said type of argument that we now see so often in politics. If a criticism is introduced, the speaker must use a civil tone of voice, present only facts, and offer an alternative. As a facilitator, if you feel emotions have gotten too high, use the bucket to stop the discussion and restore group cohesiveness.

223

The Issue or Idea Bin. The Issue or Idea Bin is a similar procedure that is meant to keep the group on task and focused on the agenda. Often times in meetings, group members will introduce an idea or issue that is important, but that is not directly related to the topic at hand on the agenda. The Idea Bin allows the team to capture the idea or issue without getting off track. Here is how it works. At the beginning of the meeting the facilitator announces that the Idea\Issue Bin will be used throughout the meeting. The facilitator explains that ideas or issues that are important, but that are not a planned part of the day's agenda, will be written down on separate sheets of paper and put in the Bin. The facilitator can write these issues and ideas down and place them in the Bin or individual team members can choose to write their ideas and then place them in the Bin during breaks or at the end of the meeting. Time permitting, the meeting facilitator can choose to go to the Bin at the end of the meeting to discuss one item or more. Bin items can also be scheduled to appear on the agenda for future meetings. Use of the Bin idea can keep a meeting on track and at the same time important ideas or issues can be recorded for possible examination and discussion at a later point.

Take Breaks. We often take a break by having everyone stand up, walk around the meeting table once and then sit in another seat. If you have an agenda item that you know will be very interesting or stimulating, consider jumping down to that item and then returning later to the planned order of your agenda items. If you are under the control of your audience, you will do whatever is necessary to keep enthusiasm and interest levels up. As your meeting progresses, consider asking your team "How are we doing?" and "Is there anything we could be doing differently to improve this meeting process?" Ensuring group member participation is critical to making your meeting successful. The more group members believe that the team participation levels are good, their input and ideas are being considered, and their questions and opinions are being addressed, the more they will assume ownership of the success and outcomes of the meeting. Going to a meeting where the manager talks at you, is not an effective meeting.

Making Meetings Interesting and Fun. Over the years, we have accumulated a number of creative ideas to keep meetings fun and interesting. Here are a few to consider for your next meeting:

- Place a lottery ticket under each person's chair. Ask everyone to reach under his or her chair at the end of the meeting.

- If you could implement one new idea, what would it be? Facilitate a group discussion on identifying and implementing a new service idea.

- Invite a customer to your meeting. Invite a customer to come and talk about his\her business.

- Role-playing: Ask staff members to role-play different situations that might occur in the office. For example, a difficult customer phone call; explaining why a customer needs title insurance; recovering from a service mistake with a customer.

- The Fake Out: At your regularly scheduled meeting time, fake your staff out by doing something completely different. For example, take them out to lunch; wash cars in the parking lot; have a local group come in for a concert; clean the reception area; or go on a picnic.

- CSI. Model a difficult title issue discussion based on the format of the popular TV show CSI.

- Computer Training: Have someone from your IT department come and give a tip on some easy, time saving procedure employees can use on their computer or a particular software application.

- Hors d' oeuvres: Provide tidbits of new information regarding title issues, news, new best practices, glimpses into the future, etc.

Meeting-in-a-bag

Several years ago, Debbie Snell at Metropolitan Title came up with the idea of a "Meeting in a Bag." The idea of a Meeting-in-a-Bag took the meeting agenda template concept one step further. It provided managers with a starter agenda, already prepared and ready to use, and it added some fun with a twist.

Working from this idea, we gathered all the managers of a title insurance agency in Hawaii together and had them plan the agenda for each month for the whole calendar year. In their instructions, they were to incorporate optional seasonal items, and planning items that occur during the year. Our idea was to print out each monthly meeting agenda that was developed and distribute them to managers in a brown paper bag, ready for use, much as if someone would receive a brown paper bag for lunch. To make the monthly meeting-in-a-bag more interesting, we asked the managers to develop a theme that would run throughout the year and be an integral component built into each meeting. Because this was a manager workshop with more than one hundred managers, we divided the group into large teams. After forty-five minutes, we had the teams present their meeting agenda for the year.

Among many great ideas, one that we liked best used the metaphor of the ocean canoe. In Hawaii, ocean canoes race from island to island, and many businesses have or sponsor a racing team. The great thing about using the ocean racing canoe as a metaphor is that each position in the canoe has a specific job, and each race has a series of stages or tactical moments. Finally, the great thing about a racing canoe is you cannot win without teamwork.

The participants in this workshop activity had a lot of fun with the meeting-in-the-bag concept and the theme. The activity sparked enthusiasm and creativity among the managers and resulted in a meeting that everyone enjoyed and judged worthwhile.

Brainstorming

The idea of brainstorming was first popularized by Alex F. Osborn in 1948. His general premise was that in groups, participants fear critical judgment about their ideas and thus self-edit themselves in terms of what they put forward. Osborn developed a process that suspended criticism and forced original ideas. We use brainstorming procedures in meetings where the purpose is to develop new ways of doing work, new solutions to common problems, and new ideas related to customer service or delivery systems.

When you use brainstorming in a meeting you create a group environment in which the rules demand that the criticism of ideas be suspended. As a creative technique, brainstorming allows that all ideas are considered legitimate and the more ideas you come up with the better. Osborn believed that it was "easier to tone down a wild idea than to think up a new one."

The procedure we follow calls for each group member to submit (write) as many ideas as they can think of in a structured amount of time. In some examples, we ask the participants to write five ideas or ten. Critical in this process is that each person must write their ideas.

In some examples, we have had the group bring a list of ideas, but experience has shown that a prepared list is not always better than a list of ideas forced into a short period. Procedurally, we write out each idea on a flip chart for all group members to see, without any discussion or criticism, and then we go back and analyze each idea, synthesizing or combining similar ideas and adjusting others eventually paring them down to those the group believes are the most promising.

Brainstorming is a great way to energize a meeting and get the creative juices flowing. We recommend the procedure to be inserted into the agenda of any meeting when a problem or issue needs to be solved or a new idea needs to be developed. The process can be carried out in a relatively short period or it can be used repeatedly. In work redesign, brainstorming can be the sole agenda item and the purpose of a meeting.

Guiding Principle

> **Brainstorming forces original ideas.**

Listed below are the steps we use for brainstorming to solve a problem or develop a new procedure, idea, or initiative.

1. Environment: Arrange to have group members sit at table conducive to good interaction and communication. Provide a pad where they can write their ideas. Position a flip chart or other suitable method to capture and display the ideas for the group.
2. Explain the purpose of the meeting and review all of the steps in the brainstorming process.
3. Instruct each person to make a list of ideas. In general requiring only one or two ideas will result in mediocre ideas. We require five to ten written ideas. Give the group five minutes to fifteen minutes to generate their list of ideas. Make sure they work independently. Make sure everyone has written ideas.
4. Using the flip chart to write, go around the group and ask each member to present one idea from their list. Record the idea for everyone to see and then move on to the next person and record their ideas.
5. Repeat this process going around the group until all ideas have been recorded.

6. If a person's idea is presented by someone else, he/she must add a new idea to his/her list.

7. At this point, some meeting facilitators ask the group to start the process over to develop a second round of ideas. The ideas generated from the second round are often more creative because they challenge people to go beyond the obvious with the added benefit that second ideas take advantage of previous ideas.

Once the list of ideas is completed, the process turns to problem solving and decision-making. Start at the beginning of your list of ideas and have the group discuss the merits (pros and cons) for each idea. The goal is to start determining which ideas are most useable given the constraints or parameters that exist. As part of this process, we may have the group rate or estimate the costs of an idea, both in dollars and in time and effort, and then we rate the benefits or impact. These ratings can be used to rank order ideas. The goal is to narrow your list down to five useable ideas. You can ask group members to rank order their preferences to determine which ideas you might turn to first. Implementation planning typically takes place in additional meetings, but you can end the brainstorming session by referring to what the next planning steps would be.

Finish on Time

Finishing your meetings on time is probably more important than starting on time. Remember that the people attending the meeting have arranged their schedule according to the agenda and schedule you provided. Ending on time, says you are organized and it says you can be depended upon. If you are running over your stated meeting time, it is better to table an item until next time. Keeping employees away from other activities they have planned on will make employees less interested in coming to your next meeting. Summarize the major decisions made and the outcomes reached in the meeting. You can call on your recorder to help with your review. Set a date on the calendar for the next meeting, if your meeting is reoccurring, and thank the team for their participation.

Evaluate Your Meetings

At the end of the meeting, consider a more formal evaluation of the meeting by your team members. You may choose to do this once a quarter or at the halfway point in a project. Return to your ground rules and ask everyone to rate on a 1-5 scale, with 5 being strongly agree and 1 being strongly disagree, each of your meeting ground rules. For example, your evaluation items could be:

1. Everyone on the team had the opportunity to speak.
2. Team members were direct and honest.
3. Team members did not hold back.
4. Team members asked questions.
5. Team members listened to each other.
6. Team members were constructively critical.
7. Team members were open to the ideas of others.
8. The team stayed on task and was focused.
9. Team members were supportive of each other.
10. The group acted well together as a team.

Additional evaluation items to consider include questions regarding the importance or usefulness of the meeting agenda items, the efficiency of the meeting, and whether the meeting decisions, outcomes, responsibilities and timelines were made clear.

Conducting Informal Meetings

We believe one of the biggest mistakes a manager can make is not meeting with employees and managers on a regular basis. As we stated earlier, being able to conduct an effective meeting is one of the most important tools a manager can use. Having said that meetings are important, not all meetings need to be formal. Being able to hold brief, informal or in-the-moment meetings is another important skill. We often talk to title department managers about "Walking the Floor" each morning. The idea is for the manager, perhaps with a cup of coffee, at the beginning of each morning, to walk around the office stopping and talking with individual employees. These informal meetings can be used to check on file progress, discuss a customer issue, take the general pulse of the office, or simply convey a general message that will also be communicated to employees using other means as well. Some managers have even been known to discuss the score of a local sports team or provide a review of a new restaurant or movie! Another idea we like is what we call "The Daily Status Update" or "Huddle." This is an informal meeting of not more than approximately 15 minutes that occurs at a pre-determined time of the day. First thing in the morning, immediately after lunch, or at the end of the day a manager conducts an informal status update. We have seen the daily status update used in title and Escrow offices. These meetings focus on the immediate issues that employees have with specific files, orders, or customers. It is also a time when a status update can be given about orders in the immediate pipeline. Because these informal meetings are scheduled by the manager to occur regularly each day, employees can look forward and anticipate having their questions answered or issues discussed at regularly occurring, consistent, frequent intervals. Daily status update meetings often save time because employees can count on their occurrence and often do not feel the need to gain access with the manager during other times of the day.

Social Networking

For today's employees, social networking and communication tools like email, Twitter, and Facebook have taken the place of actual physical meetings. Because of this, it will be natural to use these tools in addition to formal or informal meetings. Provided the word is in addition and not instead, we are in favor of using any communication tool. However, research and experience tells us that something is lost when managers only communicate with email or talks on the phone. An added positive social dimension occurs when managers and employees talk in an actual face-to-face meeting.

We hope that you can see from this chapter that we do not hate meetings. We believe in meetings both at the executive level and at the manager / employee level. In our experience, meetings can be valuable and enjoyable. We especially enjoy meetings when the meeting is planned, stays on time, covers its agenda, meets its purpose and is viewed as worthwhile and fun by the participants. We believe that if you use the ideas presented here, your employees will say, "That was a great meeting!"

TAKE AWAY ACTIVITY
CHAPTER 13
WHY MEETINGS ARE IMPORTANT

1. Write out the agenda for your next all office or team meeting.

2. Write out the agenda for the next manager or executive meeting

3. Write out the agenda for a weekly title production meeting

4. Write out the agenda for a weekly escrow meeting

5. Write out the agenda for a weekly sales meeting

6. Make a list for a different topic for 12 monthly manager meetings. Make sure the topic fits with the time of year and your planning and sales cycle.

7. Create Meeting-in-a-Bag for a weekly staff meeting.

GUIDING PRINCIPLES
CHAPTER 13
WHY MEETINGS ARE IMPORTANT

1. Conducting an effective meeting should be a part of every manager's basic skill set.

2. Good meetings require preparation.

3. Icebreakers energize meetings and make them fun.

4. Use a meeting recorder (note taker) to capture important actions and decisions. A summary of the notes should be distributed to meeting participants, including assignments and timelines. The note may be distributed to the larger workforce or all employees, but make sure the notes to be communicated are reviewed for spelling and grammar, accuracy, and content.

5. Use the Bucket rule to table an item whose discussion becomes unconstructive or is taking up too much of the agenda time.

6. Brainstorming forces original ideas.

CHAPTER 14

MAKING CHANGE PRACTICAL

One of the expectations of management is creating a stable, productive work environment. One of the expectations of leadership is causing the organization to change and grow. These sometime competing expectations must find a way to work together if an organization is to thrive.

When we ask an employee to learn a new computer system or to learn a new way to calculate a HUD, we are asking that person to change his or her behavior. Just as it is human nature to learn new things, it is also natural to resist change. In order to overcome this natural resistance, the Manager has to understand why the person is resisting and what will motivate the person to change.

In Chapter 14, we examine why employees resist change and then discuss six steps managers should follow when planning for change in title insurance companies. We end the chapter by listing ten reasons managers often fail in their change efforts.

Change in society and business is happening at a transformational pace, and an established industry like the title insurance industry is under tremendous pressure to change. Consider for a moment that most people were not using the internet, email, Google, and cell phones ten years ago. Today, a title insurance company could not exist without up-to-date computer systems, access to the internet, and cell phones. Given the revolutionary changes that the internet and technology companies like Microsoft, Apple, Google, and Facebook have caused in only ten years, the next ten years are likely to turn business practices inside out.

For the independent title agent, the last several years in real estate have been especially challenging. Real estate sales are down to historic lows and many companies have gone through waves of employee layoffs. Nonetheless, in order to stay in business, owners have been forced to keep up with new technology and new business rules at the same time competing with other companies and the underwriters. Like it or not, business practices and environment are changing and title insurance companies will either change or die.

Guiding Principle

> ### *Change or Die.*

Organizational change can be large or small, company-wide, or at the level of a procedure or the behavior of a single employee. For most people, some resistance to change is natural, regardless of the level of change, but the amount of resistance a person puts forth often is an indication of the person's perception of how the change will negatively affect them personally. For some people, the more the person perceives he/she is losing, the more he/she will fight to stay the same. In other words, the more change will affect me, the more I will resist.

Guiding Principle

> ### *In successful companies, innovation and change are a way of life.*

Resistance

A company's need to change often forces employees and managers to give up long-term, stable, patterns of work and causes them to work in new unfamiliar ways. Faced with having to learn a new way of working, some employees will jump in with both feet, some will actively resist, and most will be slow to change or passively resist. When we examine why some people "jump right in," their reasons often include they like change, they do not know how to do the work so they have little to lose, or they have no investment in the current design of the work.

When we analyze why a person is fighting change, the reasons may include one or more of the following:

Investment in the current design
- The person designed (or participated in) the current work system.
- The person took time to learn the current system.
- The person is an expert on the current system.
- The person is a top performer on the current system.

Fear
- Fear of job security – the new design may make my job unnecessary.
- Fear of looking foolish – what if I make a lot of mistakes.
- Fear of looking incapable – what if I cannot learn the new way.
- Fear of performance – I will not be able to perform as many units or as fast as I do now.
- Fear of the unfamiliar – I dislike new things or I hate uncertainty.

Loss
- Loss of control - I do not like others telling me what to do – I have to be in control.
- Loss of participation – I want the design to be my way or contain my ideas.
- Loss of freedom – I want to be free to do work my way.
- Loss of authority – I have to be in charge or the expert.

Expectations
- I will have to work harder.
- I will not have as much fun at work – I will not enjoy my work.
- I will have more (or less) responsibility.
- I will be more accountable.
- If this is successful employees will lose their jobs.

Skepticism
- I do not believe change is possible.
- I do not believe the owner is committed.
- I have been through this before and nothing happened.
- I do not believe the new way will work.
- I believe the old way is better.
- Why are we spending money on this program when I have not had a raise?

Office Politics
- I do not trust the people involved in the change effort.
- I will lose influence or authority under the new design.
- I do not trust (dislike) the people who will have new authority under the new design.
- I am jealous of who is (will be) in charge.
- My stature or position in the company will be reduced.

Having to change can make a person anxious for any number of reasons. In the face of uncertainty and anxiety, it is natural to want to cling to what is familiar and resist change. In addition to the psychological factors already listed, resisting change can be practical. Many employees have experienced a change effort that failed, wasting time and money. In the end, nothing changed and everyone went back to what he/she was doing before the project. Even when change is successful, it is often messy, time consuming, and it can be complicated and confusing. For these reasons and others, most of us would rather keep on doing what we know how to do rather than face the potential challenge and headache of changing.

Guiding Principle

Consider the source of employee motivation or fear.

Think of an employee you have managed that has resisted change. Review our list of reasons of why employees fight change and check off the factors that may have influenced your employee's behavior.

Given all the barriers to change, it is a wonder that any company changes, yet in very successful companies, innovation and change are a way of life, and they are part of the company's leadership and culture. In such companies, small changes are happening all the time, even though the company is very successful. These companies often follow the idea, "if it ain't broke, break it."

What seems most surprising is when failing companies cling to old ways and the owners and employees resist even the smallest change. Consider the example of a title department we worked in several years ago before the advent of cloud technology. The company's slow turn-time was costing them customers. When we observed the workflow, we learned that most new orders were received by fax. At various times during the day, the fax was placed in the manager's inbox. The manager then obtained a new GF number from his book, he wrote the order number on a paper order form, the form he designed and the company had been using for years. Using the information from the fax, the manager would do an initial search for priors and then based on his search add customer and property information on to the company's paper order form. Then he would send the form and the fax to a typist who entered the data into the computer. As a related step, the manager

238

would enter the GF number into a paper log, and later into an excel spreadsheet he used to track orders. In this work system, it could take more than a half a day to enter an order.

Obviously, in this example, we have inefficiencies and redundancy of function. Conceptually, the paper order form is unnecessary and the entire workflow could be completed by one person, including the search, entering data directly into the computer system, eliminating the paper forms and reducing steps and time.

In general, it is our belief that Managers should never take on more day-to-day work; rather they should manage others who perform the work. In this example, it should have been easy to get the manager to give up his work and have the typist take over the entire function. If there was going to be resistance it should have come from the typist, taking on new work and responsibilities should have at least caused the typist to ask for a raise, but in fact, the resistance came from the Manager.

By nature, the manager in this example disliked change, and he was only comfortable if he did most of the work himself. Also, he did not like typing on the computer and he did not like the title software, so having the typist entering the data he had hand written on a form saved him time and meant he did not have to learn the computer software. In practical terms, he could work the way he always had, and he was quick, efficient, and productive. On the down side, the typist's talent and ability were being underutilized; the manager was overworked and not able to use the computer system fully. In total, the work system was inefficient and costly.

In this example, when the manager was asked to change the way he did work, he flatly refused and resisted every effort to change. Ultimately, we were able to help the owner and successfully redesign the work, but the inability to involve the manager in the process of change taught us a number of lessons.

Change Process (Six Steps)

Next, we look at a six-step process that identifies what leaders can do to make their change efforts successful.

Step One: Know what and why you are changing. The larger the change effort, the more times the leader will have to explain what we are doing and why. For example, one time, we asked an employee to stop using Word Perfect and start using Word, and the first thing the employee asked was "Why?" How you answer this basic question may determine the level of resistance you encounter. Consider the following answers:

1. We are asking you to change, because the boss (the owner) said so.
2. We are asking you to change, because I (the Manager) said so.
3. We are asking you to change, because I and everyone else uses Word and we have to convert all of your WP files to Word (i.e., your work causes others an inconvenience).
4. We are asking you to change, because Word is easier to teach to new employees and we have decided that new employees will use Word. Besides, most new employees already use Word.
5. We are asking you to change, because consultants have told us using Word will make you more efficient and more productive.
6. We are asking you to change, because Word comes in the office package we have to buy, so WP is an extra cost.

When you consider the reason for change, you have to consider the source of motivation or fear into which you are tapping. Telling a person, he must change because "the Owner or Manager says so," is using authority and probably fear of unemployment as a reason. Telling an employee, they must change because it will make it easier for others; feels like you are trying to create a level of guilt and hoping for a level of altruism as motivation. Telling a person that it is easier to teach, makes sense, except the employee already has learned a way of working. His answer will be "go ahead, teach the new people and leave me alone." Similarly, claiming that a new way of working is cheaper or will make a person more productive translates into "we want to make more money and we want you to work harder." All of these explanations will cause resistance. The explanation that follows, combines several elements and builds a rationale, it tells a story, and explains why:

The owner believes it is critical employees (and customers) are communicating through the same software. To achieve this goal, we are asking everyone to shift over from WordPerfect to Word by the end of the year. Here are the reasons Word is being selected over WordPerfect. First, Word comes as part of the MS Office package, which the company already has to buy. Second, most employees already know how to use Word, so training cost and time are reduced. Third, the newest version of Word has been shown to save a number of processing steps, making it easier to use than WordPerfect and it is used by more businesses and customers. For these reasons, the company has adopted Word as its standard and all employees are being asked to use it by the end of 2010.

Notice how this explanation (the story) has two parts, what is expected and why.

Step Two: Know who is on your side. In every change effort, there are employees who will work with you; those who will promote change and those who will support change, and then there are those who will fight you every inch of the way. Although some resistance is natural and to be expected, it is useful to understand who is ready for change and who will work with you. The following checklist is a simple way to evaluate the readiness of your employees. For each employee, answer "Yes" or "No" to the ten questions. Tally the number of "Yes" checks the person receives. The greater the number of "Yes" checks, the greater that person's readiness for change. Add the totals for each of the employees you assess, convert your results to percentages, and you can translate individual readiness into your company's overall readiness for change.

Once you know who will support change, you will be in a much better position to decide how to move forward. For example, consider the employee who believes in the need for change, but who does not believe change is possible. For this employee a few quick successes (changes) may be enough to win the employee over. Whereas the employee who does not believe in the need for change, has actively resisted past change efforts, and does not believe change is possible, will be a very different problem.

For those employees who have a high number of "Yes" checks (e.g., seven or more), consider making the person a key member of your change effort, part of your "change team." For example, involve them as a project leader, place them on change committees, or go to them to enlist their ideas and ongoing support.

Readiness for Change	Yes	No
1. The Employee agrees with the need for change or is dissatisfied with the work		
2. The Employee accepts change readily – has promoted or supported past changes		
3. The employee believes change is possible		
4. The employee will support the change effort if his\her work is not affected		
5. The employee will support the change effort, even if his\her work is affected		
6. The employee will not actively oppose change efforts		
7. The employee will not passively resist change (e.g., resist in the background)		
8. The employee is able and confident in his/her current work		
9. No coaching or training will be necessary with this employee		
10. The employee is already changing		

For employees who support change, are confident in their current work, and will not need training, or are changing already, there is little need to over sell or over train, rather these employees should be used to help sell or train others. These employees might be in the key employee group.

For employees who support change, but are not confident in their current work, or who will need training, the issue is not convincing them, the issue is getting them trained and on board. These employees might be in the first group to be trained. If you conduct a pilot group, they might be in the pilot.

For employees who receive four or five "No" checks, you may want to consider working with them individually to explain how the change will affect them, what will be expected, and how they will need to support the change effort.

In some cases, you should consider the tactic of giving a passive resister responsibility to help shape your change efforts. In many instances, if you give someone an active role in the change effort, you will channel their energies in a more positive direction. Employees who are involved in planning change solutions are more likely to gain ownership, interest and investment in making change successful. However, highly vocal critics, and employees with a high level of authority and a history of active resistance should not be considered in this role.

Guiding Principle

Give passive resisters an active role in the change efforts.

If you have an employee who has a high number of "No" checks (e.g., eight or more), that employee may not be a good fit with your company in the future. It will be important to evaluate how their work, or any resistance on their part, can be tolerated. Like the manager in our earlier example, the truth is there are people whom you will have to work around.

Step Three: Form a change team. Enlist key employees to help lead the way. Regardless of the nature of your change effort, having a group of interested and creative employees who will help design, lead, and implement change is important. In general, the larger the scale of change, the more people involved in the effort. If your

243

change effort is company-wide, for example, installing a new software platform, you will need representatives from every function in the company in addition to technologists. If you are changing the work in one unit or department, for example, changing how a commitment is created, you might only involve members from the title department, although our experience suggests that including representatives from other functional areas can be important.

In some instances, the change may involve changes in dress, demeanor, or behavior. In most companies, such changes are handled as a matter of policy and are explained and trained in the new employee handbook and/or orientation. Nevertheless, if you are asking employees to give up their covered parking spots, it will be important to involve key employees in the decision! Finally, if the change involves a single employee, only the person and his/her manager should be involved in the effort.

Guiding Principle

> **Solicit employee ideas to gain greater investment in change.**

Regardless of the level of change, remember, if you solicit employee input and use employee ideas, they will be more invested in achieving successful outcomes and proud of their accomplishments. When you create a change team, consider these guidelines:

1. The owner, CEO, office or team leader must sanction the team. This means publicly announcing support and direction for the team and communicating the purpose and authority of the team to other employees.
2. The leader must stay connected to the team. You cannot simply appoint a team and then walk away. You need to be interacting with the group frequently, asking for feedback, and continuing to support the group.
3. The leader of the team must be a good facilitator and taskmaster. We recommend that new workflow design teams follow a twelve-step process that has proven successful with our clients.
4. The employees who will be affected by change initiatives must have representation on the team. If this is a company-wide or

office-wide change initiative, assign employees from the different functional areas.

5. Decision makers must be on the team. Decision makers act as good sounding boards regarding the practicality of specific ideas and offer immediate sanction. The team should be composed of a good mix of creative talent, planners and doers.

Step Four: Develop a communication plan. Having a communication process is a critical step. Here are twelve actions you should consider in developing an effective communication plan:

*   Define the need for change, explaining what needs to change and why. Provide a rationale, goals, and expected outcomes.
*   Create a vision of what the future will look like with the changes in place.
*   Create a sense of urgency by pointing to market conditions and competition.
*   Clarify leader support; make sure the leader(s) have an active, visible role.
*   Meet with key people to solicit support and discuss plans.
*   Solicit additional ideas and input from a cross section of the employees.
*   Solicit customer input.
*   Demonstrate that employee and customer input are being used.
*   Provide communication updates on progress frequently.
*   Do not rely solely on electronic communications; conduct one-on-one employee meetings, and group meetings to discuss the project.
*   Once implementation had started, identify and celebrate initial successes, intermediate milestones, and goals reached.
*   Communicate what adjustments are being made as to the results and evaluation of implementation progresses.

The last thing you want is a group of employees meeting behind closed doors, planning change, without communicating regularly what they are doing and why. Several years ago, we facilitated a large-scale workflow redesign project in a title department. To plan the work redesign, we formed a seven-person team with managers and key employees.

Guiding Principle

Communicate throughout implementation.

The group met regularly each month discussing changes that were designed to improve commitment turn-time. Unfortunately, the project got off to a rough start with the general staff in an uproar fearing loss of jobs and office closings and we soon realized that poor communication was at the center of the problem. We quickly acted to put a comprehensive communication plan in place.

Step Five: Start small. If you can, we recommend starting small. Even when the project is large, we try to divide the change initiative into stages or increments. If possible, with large-scale change, we try to test our ideas on a smaller scale. For example, implementing new procedures as a pilot test in one unit or with one team or office is a good way to iron out any flaws or bugs in a new workflow design. A pilot test helps you identify problems and corrects them before implementation (and disaster) on a larger scale.

Guiding Principle

Start small and test to find bugs and create momentum.

Starting in an incremental way is also a good way to build momentum. For example, use the pilot as the showcase for the positive changes that will be produced and the employees and managers involved in the pilot can become supporters and spokespersons for change throughout the remaining levels of the company. As more and more units or offices come on-line, and as you meet your intermediate objectives and milestones, momentum will naturally increase until you have ultimately met your end goal.

Guiding Principle

Celebrate small and large accomplishments early and often.

Starting small can also mean simply limiting the scope of the change you are considering. Here is a list of five small, rather simple, incremental ideas, title insurance agencies can consider for change:

1. Create a consistent impression in each lobby or retail space that you have. This means things like: color schemes; signage; furniture, customer amenities and services, and the ways customers are greeted and served as they enter your space.
2. Eliminate one or more redundant workflow procedure or process.
3. Have all employees who answer customer calls, answer the phone in the same way and route customer inquiries in the same way.
4. Have managers hold monthly meetings that follow agreed upon similar agenda. Communicate the results of each meeting.
5. Develop an employee professional dress look. For example, the use of shirts with company logo's.

Although larger change efforts in title insurance agencies can be more complicated and involve many more steps and levels of people and systems, moving forward with these projects can also be considered and developed using incremental steps. Here is a list of larger scale change initiatives that title agents should be considering, if they have not already:

1. Develop standards for quality, turn-time, productivity and customer satisfaction and work with managers to enforce the standards and train accountability.
2. Centralize order entry and customer service functions.
3. Centralize title production and combine search, exam and commitment production functions.
4. Centralize escrow processing and post-closing functions.
5. Develop off hour\off site-closing procedures, including weekends, incorporating new electronic technology.

6. Map out your customer points of contact and develop a "WOW" customer service approach.
7. Flatten and streamline your management structure.

Step Six: Monitor and evaluate your progress on an ongoing basis. Whether you are coaching a single employee on phone etiquette or changing the software platform used in a company of 300 employees, your change effort consists of three critical parts: goal, plan, and outcome. Every change plan should include how you will evaluate both progress towards a goal and results.

Wherever possible, the evaluation should include objective measures or outcome measures. For example, orders, closings, and revenue can be measured (counted) in different periods, daily, weekly, or monthly. In addition, these measures can be assigned to products, units and individuals. Based on these outcomes we can determine individual and unit productivity, turn-time, error rate, labor ratio, income per order, and orders and closings per day.

Using measures that are more subjective, we can use a survey to assess employee and customer satisfaction. Somewhat less objective but still important assessments can be obtained from your employees and customers in the form of comments or complaints, or in interviews.

Whenever possible, measurement and evaluation should start before the project begins, occur throughout the life of the project and continue for a defined period after the implementation is completed. Think of your project as having four measurement phases:

1. Baseline – the period before any planning
2. Awareness – after the goals are revealed and during the planning – before implementation
3. Implementation - During training and while change is occurring
4. Follow-up - after implementation is completed

Establishing a baseline or starting point for your evaluation, simply means documenting your performance before starting your change project. For example, if you are going to improve your title turn time, you will want to measure turn-time for a period (3 months) before the plan is announced.

Research suggests that for some people, making expectations clear (awareness and commitment) may be sufficient (for a time) to improve performance, so it is useful to measure performance before and after awareness and during planning but before any intervention. If the intervention is costly, it is sensible to determine whether simply telling the employees to change and measuring performance is sufficient to bring about a meaningful change.

For example, in a company where sales are made over the phone, the sales staff were told the company wanted to improve basic phone sale skills and staff were going to receive a workshop on sales. The standard policy of the company has been to monitor sales calls for the last year. They are told they will be evaluated on three measures: obtaining and using the customer's name; obtaining the customer's phone number and email address; and, sales on the first call. Sales calls were monitored using these measures, for a period before the program was announced, to establish a baseline. After announcing the project goals, phone calls were sampled for a week. Essentially, employees are told what is expected and a week of calls is used to determine the effects of making expectations clear. After a week, the training is given. Once the training is given, the calls are monitored for another week, and then again three months later. Because we are able to assess performance before and after our implementation, we can determine the cost benefit of any future sales training.

Frequent measurement and consistent monitoring of results and progress is important and you will want to include news of your accomplishments in your communication updates. When your change project is operational and all the new procedures and system changes are in place, you can assess the progress you have made by comparing your baseline measures with your new measurement results taken after full implementation.

Guiding Principle

> **If you measure it, they do it.**

In general, measurement is an afterthought, it is the last item considered in planning change, or measures are added after the project is finished. In our experience, measurement needs to be one of the first steps in the process. An old adage says, "If you measure it, they do it." We could not agree more.

Why change efforts fail

Whether you are planning some sort of incremental change or a larger scale project, failure to change usually results when one or more of the following have not been considered.

- Leadership for the initiative is delegated.
- Management is not visible during the life of the project.
- Communication is insufficient.
- The plans for change are conceived behind closed doors.
- Staff perceives the change is not critical.
- Alternative implementation plans are not fully explored.
- Change implications are not taken into account.
- Resistance to change is misdiagnosed.
- Tracking, monitoring and evaluation are absent.
- Additional or continued training and coaching are needed.

Guiding Principle

Change fails when leadership is delegated.

TAKE AWAY ACTIVITY
CHAPTER 14
MAKING CHANGE PRACTICAL

1. Review our list of why change efforts fail. Can you identify reasons your past change efforts have failed in some way?

2. Looking ahead to change in your title insurance company, what steps will you need to take to ensure greater success in the future.

GUIDING PRINCIPLES
CHAPTER 14
MAKING CHANGE PRACTICAL

1. Title companies will either change or die.

2. In very successful companies, innovation and change are a way of life.

3. When you consider change, factor in the source of employee motivation or fear.

4. Give passive resisters an active role in shaping the change efforts.

5. Solicit employee input and ideas to gain greater investment in change.

6. Communication is a key factor; communicate at the start and often throughout implementation.

7. Start incrementally or use a pilot test to find bugs and create momentum.

8. Celebrate small and large accomplishments early and often as you implement change.

9. Change efforts fail when leadership is delegated.

10. If you measure it, they do it.

POST SCRIPT

HELP ALONG THE WAY

We started this book by saying that leadership is about change. We also said that as a leader and manager your job is *Finding the Right Path*. We have worked with many title insurance leaders and managers throughout the country and know the right path for change for one leader is not always the same path taken by another. We also have learned that once you start down a path to change, new choices emerge that would not have been possible, if you had not started down a path.

During our twenty years working in the title insurance industry, we have gone down many paths and learned as much as we taught. Because our careers consulting in the title insurance industry began with a consulting contract with Chicago Title, we would be remiss in not mentioning the support and friendship we received from Alan Prince, Chris Abbinante, and Burt Rain among many others.

In the Midwest, we have worked with a number of great companies and presidents, including: Ken Lingenfelter and his team at Metropolitan Title and LPE, Mark Myers at Meridian Title, and Frank Pellegrini at Prairie Title in Chicago, Illinois. In Michigan, CEO Ken Lingenfelter was a member of a special program for agents put on by Chicago Title in 1994. After the program, Ken asked if we could help implement the ideas he had learned in the program. To start, we met with Ken and his executive team to develop a vision and values statement for the company. At the time, Ken had some thirty offices in one state, Michigan. Ken's company had gone from one employee to over three hundred in less than ten years. As often happens, the company outgrew its infrastructure and was missing some of the fundamentals of a larger company. CBA's role was to help Ken and his executive team find the path for the next stage in the company's growth. Ten years later, the company was in eleven states and had more than eight hundred employees. During that time, we helped to evaluate new acquisitions, facilitated the company's annual executive retreat, participated in monthly executive meetings, developed a compensation system, implemented a company-wide marketing planning process, and provided seminars on management and leadership. Working with Ken and his executive team: Dennis Lintemuth, Terry Brown, Debi Snell, David Smessaert, Dave Walker, and Robin Gilroy among many others, was a great experience and CBA was proud to be part of the growth of one of the largest independent title insurance companies in the United States. One truism that Ken says he learned from CBA and we learned every day working with Ken was, "If it isn't written it isn't a plan."

In Indiana, we worked with CEO Mark Myers at Meridian Title who asked us initially to help train the company's managers. Because the training process revealed manager strengths and weaknesses, the path we helped Mark and his team choose eventually led to the re-organization of his management structure and processes and the clearer definition of manager roles, responsibilities, and lines of accountability, including the development of a performance management system for the entire company. In the years that followed, we helped define and implement a sales and marketing approach and a new manager-training program. In working with Meridian, we always thought we learned as much or more from Mark Myers, David Dunbar, Laura Francesconi, Debbie Collins and the whole Meridian Title Team as they learned from us.

In Texas we have worked with a number of larger than life companies and people, including the Rattikin family, Jack Jr., Jack III, and Jeff in Ft. Worth, Alex Harris in Corpus Christi, Paul Rodriguez in McAllen, John Martin in El Paso, Jack Rogers in San Antonio, and George Mike Ramsey in Dallas. In College Station Texas, we worked with CEO Celia Goode-Haddock at University Title. Initially, Celia asked us to help her decide whether she needed to move to a new location or expand in her current location. The path that we helped Celia choose led her and her team to redesign her entire workflow, thereby improving the company's efficiency and the use of her available space, eliminating the need to move to a new location. Because gaining customer insights and ideas were critical to the redesign of workflow, Celia's path led her to implementing a new customer interviewing, discovery process with her customers and eventually a new sales and marketing approach.

On the east coast, we worked in underwriter direct operations, corporate title insurance agencies, and attorney based title insurance agencies. In New York City, we had the great pleasure to work with Steve Day, Marion Latham, Ted Werner, and the entire crew of very talented direct managers and agency staff. In upstate New York, Frank Carroll was a true supporter. From our New York and New Jersey clients, we learned the title business can be very different even within a state.

On the west coast, we had the pleasure of working with Bill Massey at Chicago Title right at the time Chicago Title had acquired Ticor and Security Union. Taking over the two brands Bill had acquired two very different, but equally competitive managers in Portland. Bill believed that so long as a manager was meeting his/her goals and there were no employee problems, then he/she should be left alone. However, if a manager fell below his performance goals, then he acquired a partner, Bill Massey. The threat of "you don't want me as a partner" did more to motivate his managers than any incentive. This was a simple tactic we learned and we continue to use it as a principle.

We offer these examples simply to say that innovation, change, and business success requires leaders and managers to find the right path and to make important choices along the way. As we have discussed in this book, we believe the starting point is assessing your organization. After that, the path is up to you. If you lack vision and goals, start by setting a clear direction. Perhaps your company lacks the metrics needed to manage by the numbers or perhaps you need to evaluate employee performance. Whatever path you take, developing your team and improving your employee culture by managing problems and providing support and guidance when needed will always be good advice. In writing this book, we hope that you can use the ideas in it to find your right path to success and that along your way, as you learn new ways to lead and manage, you will share them with us.